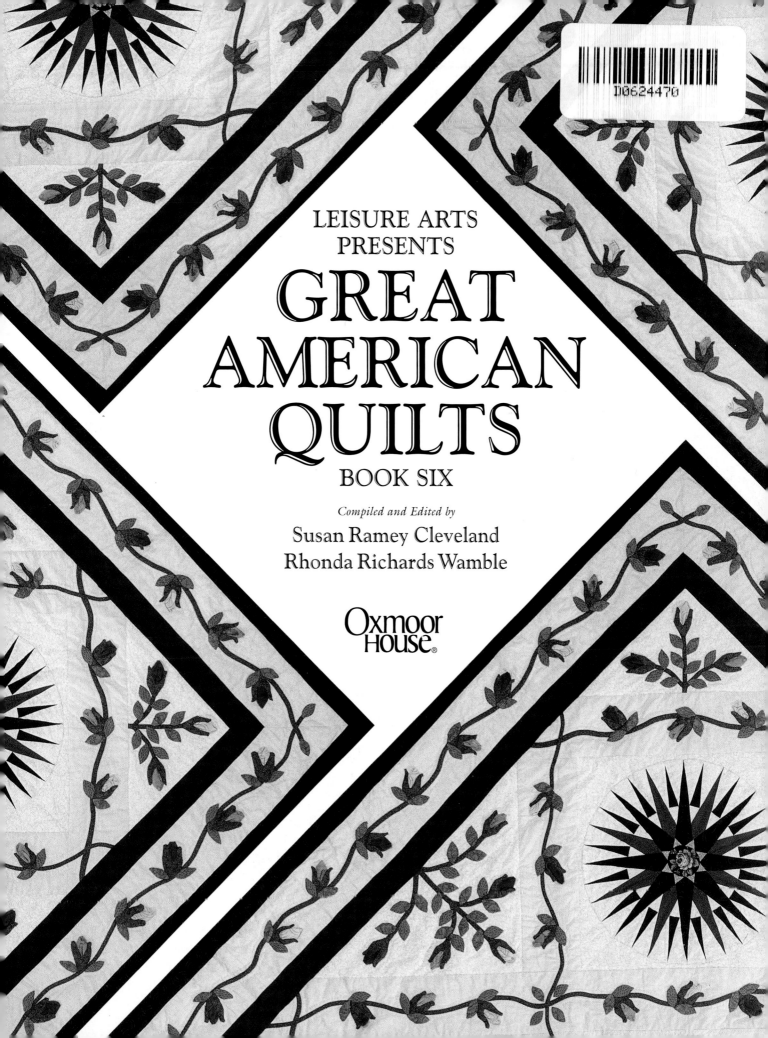

LEISURE ARTS
PRESENTS

GREAT AMERICAN QUILTS

BOOK SIX

Compiled and Edited by

Susan Ramey Cleveland
Rhonda Richards Wamble

Oxmoor House.

Great American Quilts Book Six
©1998 by Oxmoor House, Inc.
Book Division of Southern Progress Corporation
P.O. Box 2463, Birmingham, AL 35201

Published by Oxmoor House, Inc., and Leisure Arts, Inc.

Library of Congress Catalog Card Number: 86-62283
ISBN: 0-8487-1695-7
ISSN: 1076-7673
Manufactured in the United States of America
First Printing 1998

Editor-in-Chief: Nancy Fitzpatrick Wyatt
Senior Crafts Editor: Susan Ramey Cleveland
Senior Editor, Editorial Services: Olivia Kindig Wells
Art Director: James Boone

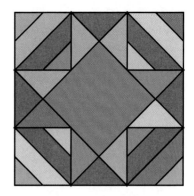

Great American Quilts Book Six

Editor: Rhonda Richards Wamble
Copy Editor: Susan S. Cheatham
Editorial Assistants: Lauren Brooks, Cecile Nierodzinski
Technical Writer: Laura Morris Edwards
Director, Production and Distribution: Phillip Lee
Associate Production Manager: Theresa L. Beste
Production Assistant: Faye Porter Bonner
Designer: Barbara Ball
Illustrator: Kelly Davis
Publishing Systems Administrator: Rick Tucker
Senior Photographer: John O'Hagan
Photo Stylist: Linda Baltzell Wright

We're Here for You!
We at Oxmoor House are dedicated to serving you with reliable information that expands your imagination and enriches your life. We welcome your comments and suggestions. Please write us at:
Oxmoor House, Inc.
Editor, *Great American Quilts*
2100 Lakeshore Drive
Birmingham, AL 35209
To order additional publications, call 1-205-877-6560.

EDITOR'S NOTE

The techniques featured in this year's special chapter, "Quick-Method Quilts," won't give you more time—they'll just make the most of the quilting time you have. You'll find quick-pieced triangles in Susan Adler's *Peanut Butter and Jelly*, fast chain piecing in Mary Jane Shank's lovely *Boston Commons*, and more.

Get ready for some awesome offerings in "Quilts Across America." The artistry of Mabeth H. Oxenreider's *Friendship Garden* and the use of color in Joe Horansky's *Clambake* will amaze you.

If, like Marion Roach Watchinski, you love the look of antique scrap quilts, don't miss her *Pine Burr*, just one of the many stars in "Traditions in Quilting."

Sometimes many hands make not only light but also lovely work—as this year's bee quilters prove. You won't be able to take your eyes off of such masterpieces as the Letort Quilters' *Mariner's Rose Compass* or *Rhapsody in Blue*, made by the Blue Valley Quilt Guild.

"Designer Gallery" features some outstanding artists, such as Eileen Sullivan, who gives you a taste of Impressionism with *Remembering Monet*, and Michele Hardy, who proves art can be fun with *Day Star*.

Thank you for joining us as we celebrate America's premier quilts and quilters. We hope you find in this collection, and in the quiltmakers' stories, something that touches your heart and prompts you to pull out your fabric stash and create a great American quilt of your own.

Quick-Method Quilts

Quilts Across America

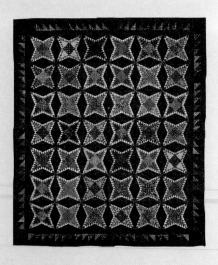

Traditions in Quilting

*B*ee Quilters

*D*esigner Gallery

*Q*uilt Smart

Quick-Method Quilts

Peanut Butter and Jelly

Boston Commons

Twinkling Stars

Night and Noon Stars

Triple Irish Chain Racing Quilt

Odd Fellows March

Susan Adler
Randolph, New Jersey

*S*usan Adler does not come from a long line of quilters. Her mother didn't quilt, and neither did her grandmothers. They were all knitters.

"I make quilts for the sheer enjoyment and challenge of it."

Susan discovered quilting by accident about nine years ago.

"One of my teenage daughters suggested we get a sewing machine," she explains, "mostly, I think, so she could sew patches on jeans."

Without a lot of excitement, Susan began to shop for a sewing machine. Her quest took her to several quilting and fabric shops. It was the fabrics that hooked her—bolt after bolt of beautiful colors and textures.

"In a ridiculously short time, I amassed a first-class collection of fabric, bought a Bernina 1530, and started making quilts," she says.

Peanut Butter and Jelly
1996

The brilliant colors and visual texture exemplified in this quilt are why Susan Adler fell in love with quilting.

"When I saw all those bolts of beautiful, enticing fabric, I was hooked," she says.

Susan makes mostly wall hangings, although she has made a bed-size quilt for each of her two daughters. She prefers machine piecing because it quickly gets her to the part she enjoys most—hand quilting. "Frenetic piecing, contemplative quilting," says Susan.

Peanut Butter and Jelly has been exhibited in a number of shows and has won several ribbons, including an honorable mention for use of color at the Mid-Atlantic Quilt Festival in Williamsburg, Virginia, in 1996.

Peanut Butter and Jelly

Finished Quilt Size
52" x 44"

Number of Blocks and Finished Size
21 Large Pinwheels   5⅞" x 5⅞"
44 Small Pinwheels   3" x 3"
44 Border Pinwheels   4" x 4"

Fabric Requirements
1¾ yards total assorted gold prints for blocks
1¾ yards total assorted purple prints for blocks
½ yard black with orange dots for setting triangles
¼ yard dark print for border
¾ yard dark print with brights for binding
3½ yards dark tapestry print for backing

Pieces to Cut
Assorted gold prints
- 21 (3⅞" x 7¾") rectangles for large pinwheels
- 44 (2⅞" x 5¾") rectangles for border pinwheels
- 44 (2⅜" x 4¾") rectangles for small pinwheels

Assorted purple prints
- 21 (3⅞" x 7¾") rectangles for large pinwheels
- 44 (2⅞" x 5¾") rectangles for border pinwheels
- 44 (2⅜" x 4¾") rectangles for small pinwheels

Black with orange dots
- 1 (9½"-wide) crosswise strip. Cut strip into 4 (9½") squares. Cut squares in quarters diagonally to make 14 (plus 2 extra) side setting triangles.

- 1 (5½"-wide) crosswise strip. Cut strip into 2 (5½") squares. Cut squares in half diagonally to make 4 corner setting triangles. Trim after joining if necessary.

Dark print for border
- 4 (1⅞"-wide) crosswise strips. Cut 2 (1⅞" x 41¾") top and bottom border strips and 2 (1⅞" x 36¼") side border strips.

Quilt Top Assembly
1. Choose 1 gold print rectangle and 1 purple print rectangle in matching sizes. Referring to *Quilt Smart* on page 11, use quick-piecing method for half-square triangles to draw grid, stitch, and cut to make 4 pinwheel units. For Large Pinwheels, draw 3⅞" grid squares. For Small Pinwheels, draw 2⅜" grid squares. For Border Pinwheels, draw 2⅞" grid squares. Join as

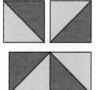

Pinwheel Block Assembly Diagram   *Pinwheel Block Diagram*

shown in *Pinwheel Block Assembly Diagram* to make 1 Pinwheel block.

2. Make 21 (6⅜") Pinwheel blocks, 44 (4½") Pinwheel border blocks, and 44 (3½") Pinwheel blocks.

3. Join 4 (3½") Pinwheel blocks as shown in *Pinwheel Quad Block Assembly Diagram* to make 1 (6⅜") Pinwheel quad block. Make 11 Pinwheel quad blocks (*Pinwheel Quad Block Diagram*).

4. Lay out 6⅜" Pinwheel blocks and Pinwheel quad blocks as shown in *Quilt Top Assembly*

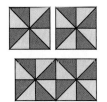

Pinwheel Quad Block Assembly Diagram

Pinwheel Quad Block Diagram

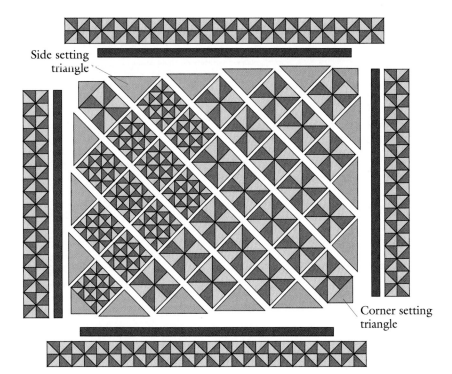

Diagram with side and corner triangles. Join in diagonal rows; join rows to complete quilt center.

5. Add 41¾" dark border strips to top and bottom of quilt. Repeat with each side border.

6. Join 9 (4½") Pinwheel blocks into a strip. Repeat. Add 1 strip to each side of quilt.

7. Join 13 (4½") Pinwheel blocks into a strip. Repeat. Add to top and bottom of quilt.

Quilt Top Assembly Diagram

Quilting

Hand-quilt in spirals that resemble knife swirls.

Finished Edges

Bind with straight-grain or bias binding made from dark with brights print.

❖QUILT SMART❖

Quick-Piecing Method for Half-Square Triangles

The grid size is ⅞" larger than the finished size of half-square triangle unit. Each square in the grid makes 2 half-square triangle units.

Mark a grid on the wrong side of the lighter fabric. For 4 (2") finished squares, for example, draw 2 (2⅞") squares, drawing accurately. Draw alternating diagonal lines across these squares (shown in red in *Diagram 1*).

Layer fabrics right sides facing with the lighter fabric on top. Starting in 1 corner, stitch ¼" to the left of drawn diagonal line. Continue stitching, pivoting at corners, until you return to beginning *(Diagram 1)*. Every diagonal line will now have stitching on both sides.

Cut on every marked line. Press open to reveal half-square triangles *(Diagram 2)*.

This method works for any size and any number of triangles. For instance, to make 24

(2") finished half-square triangles, start with 8⅝" x 11½" rectangles. Draw a 3 x 4 grid of 2⅞" squares on the wrong side of the lighter fabric. Add diagonal lines that alternate in each square, as shown in *Diagram 3*. Stitch ¼" from each diagonal. Cut on all marked lines and press.

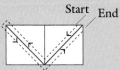

Diagram 1

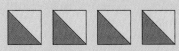

Diagram 2

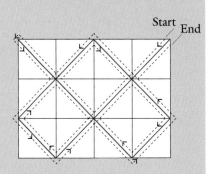

Diagram 3

11

Mary Jane Shank
Floyd, Virginia

*M*ary Jane Shank has been quilting for 40 years and has completed more than 50 quilts. "I learned to quilt at the time I got married," she says.

"I didn't dream when I took geometry in high school that it would be such a help in drafting my quilt patterns."

Log Cabin and Trip Around the World designs are her favorites. She also likes sampler quilts. Her next big project will be a queen-size sampler quilt for a cousin. She likes to machine piece and hand quilt, and often drafts her own patterns.

Mary Jane lists her occupation as homemaker—and she's not kidding. In fact, this mother of two and grandmother of four has made an art out of homemaking. She crochets and sews garments. She grows flowers and vegetables, cans and freezes, makes pickles and jelly, and even bakes her own bread.

"But quilting is my first love," she says. She adds that sometimes, she leaves off flower gardening and sewing in order to have more time to make quilts.

Boston Commons
Late 1970s

Mary Jane Shank isn't sure exactly when she made this variation of the Trip Around the World design. "It was made in the late 1970s," she says. She remembers that all the fabrics were 36"-wide cotton prints and solids.

"It took me a few years to find all the fabrics I used in this quilt," she adds. She had a definite idea of how she wanted her quilt to look. She ordered fabrics, a yard at a time, from Sears and other mail-order catalogs.

Mary Jane drew and colored her quilt design on paper, and then cut a 2½" square from sandpaper to use as a template. She cut and pieced each square separately.

We've updated Mary Jane's technique, giving you instructions for quick rotary cutting and chain piecing, options Mary Jane didn't have in the late 1970s.

Mary Jane's quilt has been in numerous shows and has won several ribbons: two blue, one red, and one white.

Boston Commons

Finished Quilt Size
99" x 113¼"

Number of Pieces and Finished Size
2,726 (2") squares

Fabric Requirements*
34 different prints:
- 11½ yards Fabric 1–light green print
- ⅛ yard Fabric 2–yellow green floral
- ¼ yard each Fabrics 3–10
- ½ yard each Fabrics 11–22
- ¾ yard each Fabrics 23–34

*See table on page 17 for colors and yardage.

Pieces to Cut
Referring to table, rotary-cut 2½"-wide crosswise strips from fabrics. Then rotary-cut strips into 2½" squares.

Quilt Top Assembly

Instructions are for chain piecing. The secret to making this quilt is to keep the squares in the correct color sequence. Stack squares on a tray or in zip-top plastic bags with labels so you can pick up the correct square as you sew.

You will chain-piece squares of the same color vertically. As you switch to a new color, you will begin to make horizontal rows, as shown in *Unit A Assembly Diagram.*

The first vertical color band is 1 square of Fabric #2, which appears at the upper left corner of Unit A. The second vertical band is 2 squares of Fabric #1, followed by 3 squares of Fabric #2, then 4 squares of Fabric #3, and so on. You will chain-piece squares of the same color band vertically. As you add each new color, you form the horizontal rows shown. The last square in the vertical color band becomes the start of a new row.

Do not cut threads between rows. This keeps them in order until the rows are joined. Do not press until unit is complete.

1. To start first row, sew 1 Fabric #2 square to 1 Fabric #1 square. Another Fabric #1 square begins the second row.

2. The third vertical color band is Fabric #2 squares.

Chain-piece 1 Fabric #2 square to right of both Fabric #1 squares. The third Fabric #2 square begins Row 3.

3. Referring to *Unit A Assembly Diagram* and Color Key, add each color band as shown.

4. When rows are complete, you will have 36 rows, all ending with a single Fabric #1 square. Clip Rows 1 and 2 from top of chain. Press seam allowances in opposite directions in each row.

5. With right sides facing, match squares on both rows at left side (they've been offset by 1 square until now). Join rows.

Vertical Color Bands

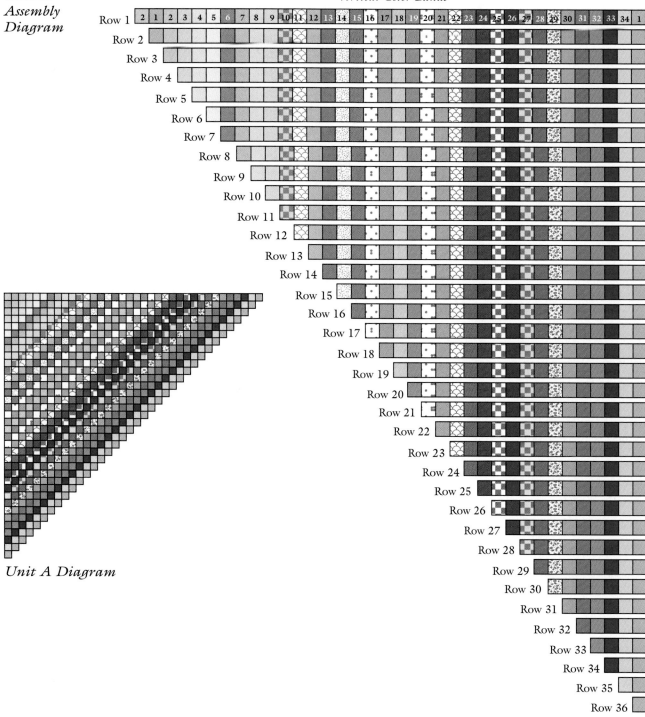

Unit A Diagram

6. Add each row, aligning squares at left side. Press seam allowances in opposite directions for each row. Continue to add rows until Row 36 (1 Fabric #1 square) is added. This completes 1 Unit A. Repeat to make 2 Unit As as shown in *Unit A Diagram*.

7. Unit B is made in a similar fashion, but the first 2 squares in each row follow a slightly different pattern. Follow *Unit B Assembly Diagram* on page 16 carefully, noting number of each fabric. There are 35 rows. Order of fabrics in first row is 3, 2, 1, 2, 3, 4, 5, 6, and so on, ending

with 33, 34, and 1. Order of fabrics in second row is 4, 3, 2, 3, 4, 5, 6, 7, and so on, ending with 33, 34, and 1, just as before. Continue in this manner through Row 33. Row 34 is 3 squares, Fabrics #1, #34, and #1. Row 35 is a single Fabric #1 square.

15

Unit B Assembly Diagram

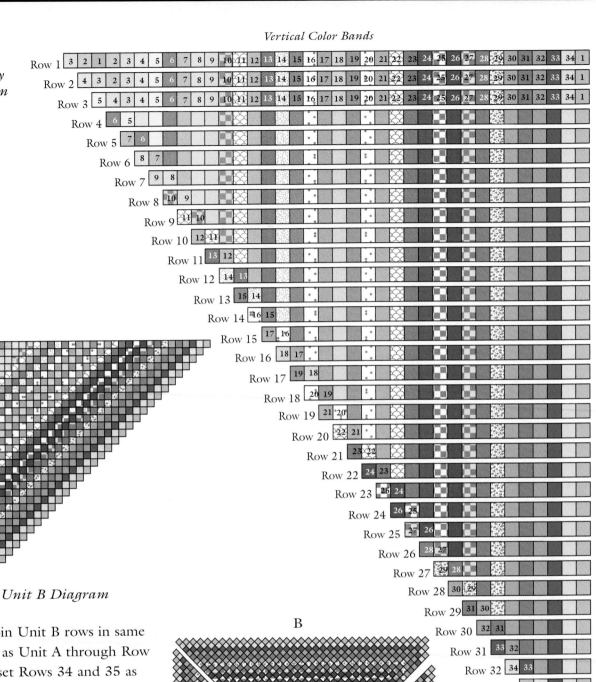

Unit B Diagram

8. Join Unit B rows in same manner as Unit A through Row 33. Offset Rows 34 and 35 as shown to make corners. This completes Unit B, as shown in *Unit B Diagram*. Repeat to make 2 Unit Bs.

9. Join Units A and B as shown in *Quilt Top Assembly Diagram*.

Quilting

Hand-quilt in-the-ditch around all squares.

Finished Edges

Bind with bias binding made from light green print.

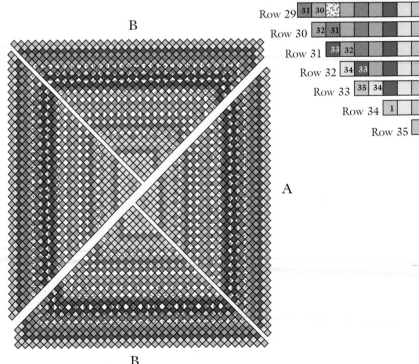

Quilt Top Assembly Diagram

❖CUTTING TABLE❖

Fabric #	Yardage	Color	Number of 2½"-wide strips to cut	Number of 2½" squares to cut from strips
1	¾ yard + 9 yards backing + 1¾ yards binding	light green print	10	152
2	⅛ yard	yellow green floral	1	14
3	¼ yard	yellow and green on white	2	18
4	¼ yard	yellow print	2	22
5	¼ yard	yellow/orange on white	2	26
6	¼ yard	solid peach	2	30
7	¼ yard	peach spots on white	3	34
8	¼ yard	peach floral on white	3	38
9	¼ yard	pink and green in a grid	3	42
10	¼ yard	pink and white on pink	3	46
11	½ yard	roses on pink grid	4	50
12	½ yard	pink print	4	54
13	½ yard	roses on white	4	58
14	½ yard	roses on pink	4	62
15	½ yard	large rose	5	66
16	½ yard	rosebuds on white	5	70
17	½ yard	pink print	5	74
18	½ yard	pink print on white	5	78
19	½ yard	medium pink and blue	6	82
20	½ yard	light floral	6	86
21	½ yard	solid lavender	6	90
22	½ yard	purple and lavender on white	6	94
23	¾ yard	purple print	7	98
24	¾ yard	dark purple and blue	7	102
25	¾ yard	purple on white	7	106
26	¾ yard	dark blue print	7	110
27	¾ yard	blue and purple on white	8	114
28	¾ yard	blue with purple	8	118
29	¾ yard	blue and white print	8	122
30	¾ yard	tan with blue	8	126
31	¾ yard	dark blue print	9	130
32	¾ yard	medium green	9	134
33	¾ yard	dark green	9	138
34	¾ yard	light with green	9	142

Carole Braig
Des Peres, Missouri

$\mathcal{W}$hile working on completing her design degree, Carole Braig became interested in fiber art, specifically quilts. "I was in a painting class," she recalls, "and the teacher said everything I did looked like a quilt with little dabs of color like patchwork." With that, Carole gave up painting and took up quiltmaking.

"I still come back to the comfortable old patterns to touch base with my grandmother's legacy."

That was 18 years ago. Since then, Carole estimates she has made about 100 quilts, mostly wall hangings.

"I do mostly non-traditional work, but I still love the traditional," she says. "I keep coming back to the comfortable old patterns to touch base with my grandmother's legacy."

Carole hand-dyes a lot of the fabric that she uses in her original works. She says she finds inspiration in many places: nature photos, children's books, art books, even vacation photos.

She says her favorite step in the quiltmaking process is design. "Once I know what it will look like, I don't want to go further," she adds.

Twinkling Stars
1997

Carole Braig's friend Ellen Sweeney was visiting her from out of state when the two decided they wanted to make a red-and-white quilt together.

"So we went quilt-shop hopping, gathering reds and small shirt prints," says Carole. During the rest of Ellen's visit, the two would stay up late in Carole's studio, taking turns cutting and sewing stars. On the morning Ellen was to leave, the two friends sat over cups of coffee and took turns claiming star blocks until they were all gone. They each planned to make more stars to have enough to finish their quilts.

"Ellen called a few days after she got home to say that it wasn't as much fun making stars alone and could I come over to her house to play."

Not able to get away at the time, Carole had to finish her quilt by herself, as did Ellen. "But she was right," says Carole. "It wasn't as much fun as making stars with a friend."

Twinkling Stars

Finished Quilt Size
92½" x 92½"

Number of Blocks and Finished Size
100 blocks   8" x 8"
(93 Variable Star blocks, 7 Double Variable Star blocks)

Fabric Requirements
5½ yards assorted red prints for blocks

5½ yards assorted light prints for blocks

2½ yards red print for borders

2½ yards cream print for borders

3¾ yards red-with-black print for borders and binding

5½ yards cream-with-red print for backing

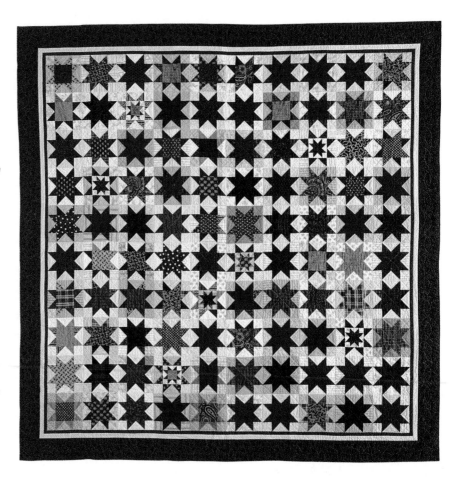

Pieces to Cut
Assorted red prints
- 11 (4½"-wide) crosswise strips. Cut strips into 93 (4½") squares (A).
- 51 (2½"-wide) crosswise strips. Cut strips into 800 (2½") squares (C) and 7 (2½") squares (E).
- 2 (1½"-wide) crosswise strips. Cut strips into 56 (1½") squares (G).

Assorted light prints
- 25 (2½"-wide) crosswise strips. Cut strips into 400 (2½") squares (D).
- 45 (2½"-wide) strips. Cut strips into 400 (2½" x 4½") rectangles (B).
- 3 (1½"-wide) crosswise strips. Cut strips into 28 (1½") squares (H) and 28 (1½" x 2½") rectangles (F).

Red border print
- 2 (1¼" x 80½") lengthwise border strips and 2 (1¼" x 82") lengthwise border strips.

Cream border print
- 2 (1½" x 82") lengthwise border strips and 2 (1½" x 84") lengthwise border strips.

Red-with-black print
- 1 yard for binding
- From remainder cut 2 (5" x 84") lengthwise border strips and 2 (5" x 93") lengthwise border strips. Reserve remainder for backing.

Quilt Top Assembly
1. To make Variable Star Block, join 2 Cs to 1 B, using diagonal-seams method (see *Quilt Smart*, page 21). Make 4 B/C units. Referring to *Variable Star Block Assembly Diagram*, join 1 A, 4 B/C units, and 4 Ds to make 1 block. Make 93 blocks as shown in *Variable Star Block Diagram*.

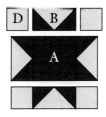

Variable Star Block Assembly Diagram

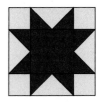

Variable Star Block Diagram

2. To make 1 *Double Variable Star Block,* use diagonal-seams method to make 4 B/C units and 4 F/G units. Join 1 E, 4 F/G units, and 4 Hs to make block center. Then add 4 B/C units and 4 Ds to complete block. Make 7 blocks as shown in *Double Variable Star Block Diagram*.

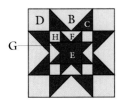

Double Variable Star Block Diagram

3. Join blocks into 10 rows of 10 blocks each as shown in *Quilt Top Assembly Diagram*, placing Double Stars as shown or as desired.

4. Join shorter red print border strips to top and bottom of quilt. Join remaining red border strips to sides.

5. Repeat with cream border and red-with-black print border.

6. To make backing, cut cream-with-red print in half to make 2 (2¾-yard) pieces. Join 1 piece of cream-with-red print to each side of 1 (18"-wide) lengthwise strip of red-with-black print. Seams will run horizontally across quilt.

Quilting

Machine-quilt in-the-ditch around all blocks and border strips. Hand-quilt Crossed Arcs Quilting Pattern, found on page 35, in outer border. Outline-quilt light triangles (B) in each block, and quilt an X across each A and D square. Quilt Double Star blocks as if they had an unpieced A square.

Finished Edges

Bind with straight-grain or bias binding made from red-with-black print.

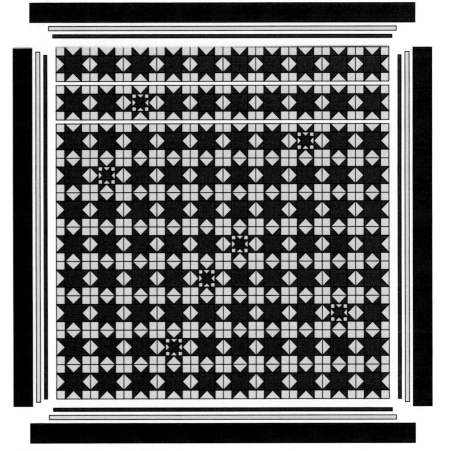

Quilt Top Assembly Diagram

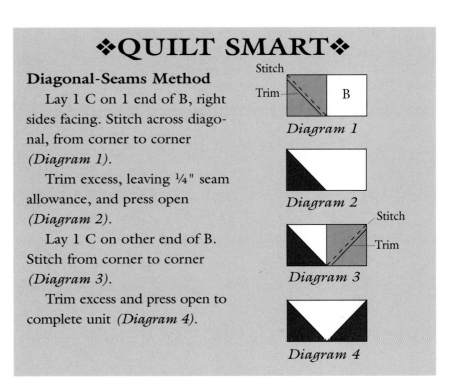

❖QUILT SMART❖

Diagonal-Seams Method

Lay 1 C on 1 end of B, right sides facing. Stitch across diagonal, from corner to corner *(Diagram 1)*.

Trim excess, leaving ¼" seam allowance, and press open *(Diagram 2)*.

Lay 1 C on other end of B. Stitch from corner to corner *(Diagram 3)*.

Trim excess and press open to complete unit *(Diagram 4)*.

Winnie S. Fleming
Houston, Texas

*Q*uilting has opened a whole new world for me," says Winnie S. Fleming. "I began quilting when my two children were small as a form of cheap therapy."

"Quilters never meet a stranger."

This new therapy soon turned into an addiction, though. Winnie has now been quilting for 15 years. After progressing from the basics to more intricate designs, she decided she wanted to share her interest with others.

"A friend owned a quilt shop near my home where I took classes," Winnie recalls. "Soon she encouraged me to start teaching. I've been teaching for 12 years, and I also lecture at area guilds."

Winnie says that she loves teaching and all the other opportunites that quilting has given her to meet quilters, whom she calls "fun people."

"Quilters never meet a stranger," she says.

Night and Noon Stars
1996

Winnie S. Fleming likes giving traditional quilt designs a new look. That's how *Night and Noon Stars* came to be. Beginning with the traditional Night and Noon block, Winnie combined strong jewel tones with black. She arranged her colors so that when the blocks were set together, they formed a field of bright stars against a black background.

Winnie is a real scrap quilt fan; she has taken part in at least 80 scrap block exchanges. "I usually like to try an unusual setting or add a pieced border to my exchange blocks so my quilts will be different," she says.

Winnie's habit of putting her own special spin on traditional patterns and exchange blocks makes her quilts unique. "People who come into the shop where I teach can often tell which quilts are mine," she says.

Night and Noon Stars

Finished Quilt Size
51" x 60"

Number of Blocks and Finished Size
20 blocks   9" x 9"

Fabric Requirements
1 yard assorted tone-on-tone bright prints for B triangles in blocks and border

2 yards assorted multi-color bright prints for A squares, striped corners, and small border squares

4 yards black for blocks, borders, and binding

4 yards rainbow stripe for backing

Pieces to Cut
Assorted tone-on-tone prints
- 56 (4¼") squares. Cut squares in quarters diagonally to make 224 quarter-square B triangles (160 for blocks, 62 for border, plus 2 extra).

Assorted multi-color prints
- 20 (4¾") squares for star centers (A).
- 66 (1½") squares for pieced border.
- 30 (1⅝"-wide) crosswise strips for striped corners.

Black
- Cut 1⅔ yards lengthwise. From this, cut 2 (3½" x 45½") lengthwise strips for inner side borders, 2 (3½" x 42½") lengthwise strips for inner top and bottom borders, 2 (3½" x 54½") lengthwise strips for outer side borders, and 2 (3½" x 51½") lengthwise strips for outer top and bottom borders.

- ¾ yard for binding.
- 20 (4¼") squares. Cut squares in quarters diagonally to make 80 quarter-square triangles (B) for blocks.
- 10 (1⅝"-wide) crosswise strips for striped corners.
- 33 (2¾") squares. Cut each in quarters diagonally to make 132 quarter-square triangles (C) for pieced border.

Quilt Top Assembly
1. Join 3 (1⅝") multi-color strips and 1 (1⅝") black strip as shown in *Strip Set Diagram*. Make 10 strip sets. Fold in half lengthwise along center seam. To cut a bias square, measure 3½" from folded seam line on each side, maintaining 45°

angles at folded corners as shown in *Cutting Diagram*. Cut along 2 sides through both layers. Do not cut along fold. Press square open. Cut 80 striped corner squares *(Striped Corner Square Diagram)*.

Strip Set Diagram

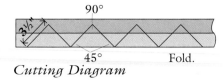

Cutting Diagram

Striped Corner Square Diagram

2. Join 1 black B and 1 bright B to make a half star point unit. Make 80 units, half with black on right and half with black on left.

3. Lay out 1 A, 4 B/B units, 4 single B triangles, and 4 striped corner squares as shown in *Night and Noon Block Assembly Diagram*. Join as shown to make 1 block (*Night and Noon Block Diagram*). Make 20 blocks.

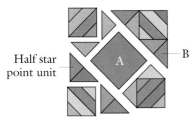

Half star point unit

Night and Noon Block Assembly Diagram

Night and Noon Block Diagram

Quilt Top Assembly Diagram

4. To make pieced border, join 1 black C triangle to 2 sides of 1 (1½") bright square as shown in *Diagram A*. Make 66 pieced-triangle units as shown in *Diagram B*. Join 14 bright B triangles and 15 pieced C units to make a strip (*Diagram C*). Make 2 strips for top and bottom borders. In same manner, join 17 bright B triangles and 18 pieced C units each to make 2 side borders.

5. Referring to *Quilt Top Assembly Diagram*, lay out star blocks in 5 horizontal rows of 4 blocks each. Join into rows; join rows to complete center.

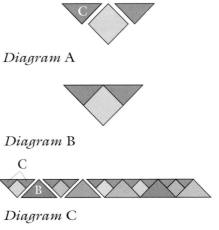

Diagram A

Diagram B

Diagram C

6. Add black inner side borders. Add top and bottom borders.

7. Add pieced borders as shown.

8. Add black outer side borders. Add top and bottom borders.

Quilting

Machine-quilt in-the-ditch around each star and around black frame of each star. Quilt in-the-ditch along border "teeth." Star centers feature a floral motif, and black borders have a wave pattern.

Finished Edges

Bind with straight-grain or bias binding made from black.

Vickie A. Ladeau-Seaver
Norwich, Vermont

Vickie A. Ladeau-Seaver is brand new to quilting. The *Triple Irish Chain Racing Quilt* is only her third piece.

"There is nothing like the feeling of putting your first block together," says Vickie. In February of 1997, she signed up for a Double Irish

"Quilting is all that's good in the world, wrapped up into one incredible experience."

Chain class at a local quilt shop. It was her first entry to a world that she soon came to cherish.

Vickie, a patient-care technician, had always loved to look at quilts and envied people who could make them. "Any time a quilt was being raffled, I'd buy at least five tickets just hoping to win it," she adds. "I don't know why it took me so long to take a class, but finally I just made up my mind to do it."

Quilting has added many positive experiences to Vickie's life. "I've met lots of new people and gained what I know will be some life-long friendships," she says. As a cross stitcher for 15 years, she had never experienced what she calls "this togetherness of strangers," referring to the kinship among quilters. Vickie is sure that she's a quilter for life. "Quilting is all that's good in the world, wrapped up into one incredible experience," she says. "I'll never stop growing in knowledge, and I'll never be alone, so long as I'm quilting."

Triple Irish Chain Racing Quilt
1997

"Michael, my second husband, introduced me to Nascar racing about three and a half years ago," recalls Vickie A. Ladeau-Seaver, "and I fell in love with it."

Racing season starts in April and ends in October. Temperatures can get pretty cold in the stands at the beginning and end of the season. Vickie decided to make a lap quilt to take to the races.

Vickie credits Michael for the final design of the quilt. "I was going to make it all black and white to represent a checkered flag," says Vickie. "But Michael suggested I make the plain blocks the colors of the other various flags used at the races."

Triple Irish Chain Racing Quilt

Finished Quilt Size
57½" x 78½"

Number of Blocks and Finished Size
35 blocks   10½" x 10½"

Fabric Requirements
8 yards black for blocks, border, backing, and binding

2 yards white for blocks

¾ yard red for blocks and borders (2¼ yards for unpieced borders)

½ yard yellow for blocks

½ yard green for blocks

½ yard blue for blocks

Pieces to Cut
Black

- 2 (2¼-yard) lengths for backing. Cut 1 panel in half lengthwise. Join 1 half-panel to 1 side of remaining length to make backing. Reserve remaining half-panel for unpieced black borders.

- 4 (2"-wide) lengthwise strips from reserved backing panel. Cut 2 (2" x 58") top and bottom border strips and 2 (2" x 76") side border strips.

- 1 (8"-wide) crosswise strip. Cut strip into 2 (8") squares for color blocks and 2 (5" x 8") rectangles for color blocks.

- 5 (2"-wide) crosswise strips. Cut strips into 34 (2" x 8") rectangles for color block strip sets and 1 (2" x 12") rectangle for color set.

- 13 (2"-wide) crosswise strips for A and B strip sets.

- 4 (2"-wide) crosswise strips. Cut strips into 72 (2") squares for chain block ends.

- 8 (2"-wide) crosswise strips. Cut strips into 2 (2" x 26") rectangles, 2 (2" x 24") rectangles, 2 (2" x 34") rectangles, 2 (2" x 40") rectangles, 2 (2" x 12") rectangles, and 2 (2" x 8") rectangles for color sets.

White

- 4 (2"-wide) crosswise strips. Cut strips into 68 (2") squares for color blocks and 1 (2" x 8") rectangle for color set.

- 1 (8"-wide) crosswise strip. Cut strip into 1 (8") square for color block and 1 (5" x 8") rectangle for color blocks.

- 12 (2"-wide) crosswise strips for A and B strip sets.

- 8 (2"-wide) crosswise strips. Cut strips into 2 (2" x 26") rectangles, 2 (2" x 24") rectangles, 2 (2" x 34") rectangles, 2 (2" x 40") rectangles, 2 (2" x 12") rectangles, and 2 (2" x 8") rectangles for color sets.

Red

• 7 (1½"-wide) crosswise strips. Piece to make 2 (1½" x 55") top and bottom border strips and 2 (1½" x 74") side border strips. If you prefer unpieced borders, cut 4 (1½"-wide) lengthwise strips from alternate yardage and proceed.

• 4 (8") squares for color blocks.

• 4 (5" x 8") rectangles for color blocks.

• 1 (2" x 24") rectangle for color set.

Yellow

• 4 (8") squares for color blocks.

• 4 (5" x 8") rectangles for color blocks.

• 1 (2" x 26") rectangle for color set.

Green

• 4 (8") squares for color blocks.

• 4 (5" x 8") rectangles for color blocks.

• 1 (2" x 40") rectangle for color set.

Blue

• 2 (8") squares for color blocks.

• 2 (5" x 8") rectangles for color blocks.

• 1 (2" x 34") rectangle for color set.

Making Color Blocks

1. Referring to *Diagram 1*, join 1 (2" x 8") black strip to each side of 1 (5" x 8") red rectangle. Cut 4 (2"-wide) strips as shown. Join 1 (2") white square to each end of 2 strips as shown in *Color Block Assembly Diagram*. Join strips to 1 (8") red

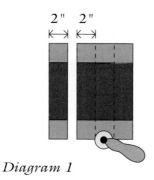

2" 2"

Diagram 1

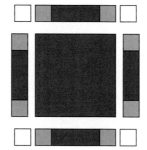

Color Block Assembly Diagram

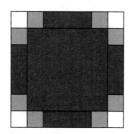

Color Block Diagram

square as shown to complete 1 red color block.

2. Make 4 red, 4 yellow, 4 green, 2 blue, 2 black, and 1 white color blocks, substituting each color for the 5" x 8" rectangle and 8" square.

Making Chain Blocks

1. Join 3 (2"-wide) black strips and 2 (2"-wide) white strips as shown in *Diagram 2* to make 1 A set. Make 3 A sets. Cut 54 (2"-wide) A strips.

2. Join 3 (2"-wide) crosswise white strips and 2 (2"-wide) crosswise black strips as shown to make 1 B set. Make 2 B sets. Cut 36 (2"-wide) B strips.

3. Join 3 A strips and 2 B strips into a center block as

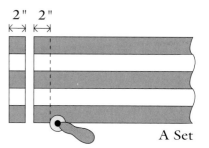

A Set

2" 2"

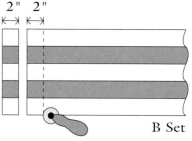

B Set

2" 2"

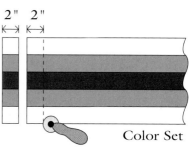

Color Set

Diagram 2

A   B   A B A

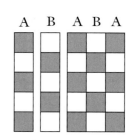

Diagram 3

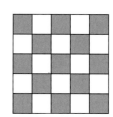

Diagram 4

shown in *Diagrams 3* and *4*. Make 18 block centers.

4. For side color strips on chain blocks, join 2 (2"-wide) black strips, 2 (2"-wide) white strips, and 1 (2"-wide) color strip in matching lengths into a color set as shown. Repeat for each color. Cut 13 (2") yellow strips, 12 (2") red strips, 17 (2") blue strips, 20 (2") green strips, 6 (2") black strips, and 4 (2") white strips. Referring to *Quilt Top Assembly Diagram* for color placement, lay out block centers with color strips. Join strips to sides of blocks as shown in *Chain Block Assembly Diagram*. Add 1 (2") black square to each end of remaining strips and add to top and bottom of blocks.

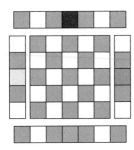

Chain Block Assembly Diagram

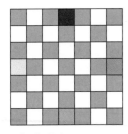

Chain Block Diagram

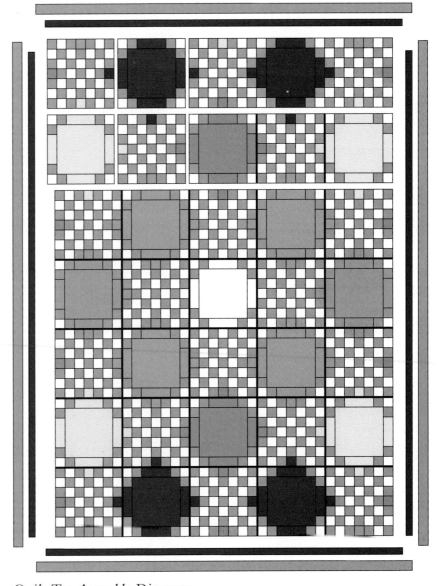

Quilt Top Assembly Diagram

5. Make 18 chain blocks as shown in *Quilt Top Assembly Diagram*.

Quilt Top Assembly

1. Lay out blocks as shown in *Quilt Top Assembly Diagram*, making sure chain blocks are turned correctly so that colors match adjoining color blocks. Join blocks into rows; join rows to complete quilt top.

2. Add 1 (1½" x 74") red border to each side of quilt. Add remaining red borders to top and bottom.

3. Add 1 (2" x 76") black border to each side of quilt. Add remaining black borders to top and bottom.

Quilting

Machine quilt in a looping allover pattern.

Finished Edges

Bind with straight-grain or bias binding made from black.

Susan Marie Stewart
Buena Vista, Colorado

*S*usan Stewart, who works in a busy travel agency, says she learned the travel business the same way she learned to quilt—"hands on."

"I have pulled out enough stitches to make a whole other quilt!"

"You make mistakes that sometimes can't be fixed," says Susan. "You learn. To be accurate in anything, you have to pay attention to details and strive for improvement."

Susan adds that quilting is her "stress buster," after a long day at work. "I can feel myself begin to wind down within minutes of picking up my quilting."

Although she admires originality, she likes traditional quilt patterns. She prefers hand work to the machine—hand piecing and quilting in a hoop—"because it's so portable and social." She adds that she likes to work on her quilts anywhere she happens to be.

"When the weather is nice, I love to sit on the porch and sew," says Susan. "But I can also work while my husband has a football game going."

Odd Fellows March
1997

Susan Stewart made this quilt for her daughter Mary Ann McClurg. It's representative of the kinds of quilts she likes to make.

"Being of Irish and Scottish descent, I love plaids," says Susan. "I picked this pattern because it made such nice sub-patterns—the big stars and the diamonds—with one simple block."

Susan entered *Odd Fellows March* in the 1997 Colorado State Fair, where it won a blue ribbon and a special award ribbon from Stearns Textiles.

A quilt is more than just fabric and stitches, Susan believes. She says, "Each quilt is a silent repository of thoughts, emotions, time, and dreams. A real piece of me, a direct link to generations yet to be."

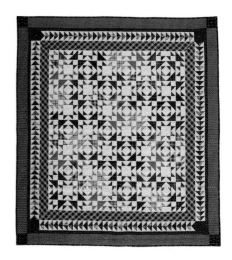

Odd Fellows March

Finished Quilt Size
82½" x 90½"

Number of Blocks and Finished Size
56 blocks   8" x 8"

Fabric Requirements
4 yards unbleached muslin for blocks and Goose Chase border

1¾ yards 60"-wide red-and-tan plaid for bias inner border (or 1½ yards 45"-wide for pieced bias border)

½ yard green plaid for pieced middle border (or 2⅜ yards for unpieced border)

¾ yard brown check for pieced outer border (or 2⅜ yards for unpieced border)

¼ yard red plaid for inner border corners

5 yards assorted dark plaids (at least 10) for blocks and Goose Chase border

1¼ yards brown plaid for outer border corners and binding

5½ yards muslin for backing

Other Materials
8 buttons for border corners

Pieces to Cut
Unbleached muslin
- 10 (2⅞"-wide) crosswise strips for Goose Chase border.
- 8 (2⅞"-wide) crosswise strips. Cut strips into 112 (2⅞") squares. Cut squares in half diagonally to make 224 half-square triangles (A).
- 14 (2⅞"-wide) crosswise strips. Cut strips into 56 (2⅞" x 8⅝") rectangles for

block A units.
- 14 (2½"-wide) crosswise strips. Cut strips into 224 (2½") squares for (B).

Red-and-tan plaid for inner border
- *If using 60"-wide fabric,* carefully cut 4 (4½"-wide) bias strips from corner to corner.
- *If using 45"-wide fabric,* cut 4½"-wide bias strips and piece to make 2 (4½" x 68") strips and 2 (4½" x 76") strips.

Green plaid for middle border
- 8 (1¾"-wide) crosswise strips. Piece to make 2 (1¾" x 78") strips and 2 (1¾" x 85") strips. If you prefer unpieced borders, use 2⅜ yards and cut 4 lengthwise strips as above.

Brown check for outer border
- 4 (4½"-wide) crosswise strips. Piece to make 2 (4½" x 75") strips and 2 (4½" x 83") strips. If you prefer unpieced borders, use 2⅜ yards and cut 4 lengthwise strips as above.

Red plaid for inner border corners
- 4 (4½") squares.

Brown plaid for border corners
- 4 (4½") squares.

Assorted dark plaids and remainders
- 10 (2⅞"-wide) assorted crosswise strips for Goose Chase border
- 56 sets of:
  *1 (2⅞" x 8⅝") rectangle for block A units.
  *1 (4⅞") square. Cut square in half diagonally to make 2 matching C triangles.

Quilt Top Assembly

1. Referring to *Quilt Smart* on page 11, mark wrong side of 1 (2⅞" x 8⅝") muslin rectangle with 3 (2⅞") squares. Match with a plaid rectangle, stitch, cut, and press to make 6 half-square triangles for A units.

2. Join 2 muslin A triangles to plaid sides of 1 A unit (*A/C Unit Assembly Diagram*). Join matching C to complete unit. Make 2 matching A-C units. Join 2 A units and 2 B squares (*B Unit Assembly Diagram*). Make 2 matching B units.

A/C Unit Assembly Diagram   *B Unit Assembly Diagram*

3. Referring to *Odd Fellows Block Assembly Diagram*, join units into halves. Join halves to complete block (*Odd Fellows Block Diagram*). Make 56 blocks.

Odd Fellows Block Assembly Diagram

Odd Fellows Block Diagram

Quilt Top Assembly Diagram

4. Arrange blocks in 8 horizontal rows of 7 blocks each, alternating direction as shown in *Quilt Top Assembly Diagram*. Join into rows; join rows to complete center.

5. Center each red-and-tan plaid border on each side of quilt and stitch. Miter corners.

6. For Goose Chase border, mark back of muslin strips with 2⅞" squares to make quick-pieced half-square triangles. Match with a plaid strip, stitch, cut, and press. If using partial plaid strips, trim muslin to the closest square and proceed. Repeat with 10 strip sets or

equivalent to make 272 half-square triangles. (There will be a few extra.)

7. Join half-square triangles to make 136 Goose Chase units as shown in *Goose Chase Border Unit Diagram*. Join to make 2 (32-unit) strips and 2 (36-unit) strips. Join 2 (36-unit) strips to sides of quilt, referring to *Quilt Top Assembly Diagram* for direction. Add 1 (4½") red plaid square to each end of remaining strips and add to quilt.

Goose Chase Border Unit Diagram

8. Center each green plaid border on each side of quilt and stitch. Miter corners.

9. Add 2 brown check borders to sides of quilt. Add 1 (4½") brown plaid square to each end of remaining brown check strips and add to quilt.

Quilting

Outline-quilt each block, with echo quilting in single A triangles. Quilt a Variable Star in each B square intersection. Repeat star in each border corner. Bias border has a Celtic Chain pattern (at right), and the Goose Chase border is outline-quilted with an echo in muslin. Quilt lengthwise channels in green border and stripes in brown check border. After quilting, add buttons to border corners.

Finished Edges

Bind with straight-grain or bias binding made from brown plaid.

Crossed Arcs Quilting Pattern for Twinkling Stars, *page 21*

Celtic Chain Quilting Pattern for Odd Fellows March *at left*

35

Quilts Across America

Joe Horansky
Brooklyn, New York

Joe Horansky was a pattern maker and production manager in New York's garment center for 40 years. When he retired, he looked forward to unlimited time to enjoy his two favorite pastimes—fishing and watching sports. Joe soon learned, however, that both of these were seasonal activities; he needed something else to fill in the gaps.

"Quilting has given me the opportunity to share the craft with my wife and given us a new togetherness."

"I became interested in quilting simply by watching my wife make quilts," says Joe. He felt that his experience making garment patterns should make the transition to quilting an easy one. "I was already comfortable using a sewing machine and cutting fabric," he says.

"Quilting has given me the opportunity to share the craft with my wife and given us a new togetherness," Joe says. Joe and Ruby, members of the Empire Quilters Guild of New York City, hold the distinction of being that guild's first quilting couple. They love going to quilt shows, especially if their quilts are being shown. "We usually come back with new energy and new ideas," says Joe.

Clambake
1996

Although Joe Horansky has been quilting for only about three years, he is already being recognized as a prize-winning quilter. *Clambake*, his log cabin variation wall hanging, won an honorable mention at the Empire Quilters Guild's 1997 show in New York City.

Joe says his inspiration for *Clambake* came from reading books on log cabin variations and their possibilities. "I designed it to use wide and narrow log cabin strips and the variations I could develop," says Joe. "I also wanted to experiment with colors I had never used."

Fabrics for the quilt came from the couple's shared collection and from used garments, linens, and table napkins.

Clambake

Finished Quilt Size
48" x 48"

Number of Blocks and Finished Size
64 blocks   5½" x 5½"

Fabric Requirements*
1½ yards total 6 assorted orange prints and solids for blocks

1 yard total 6 assorted green prints for blocks

¾ yard total 4 assorted light tan prints for blocks

1½ yards orange print for borders and outer block rows

1 yard green print for binding

3 yards tan with multi-print for backing

*See Pieces to Cut for fabrics needed.

Pieces to Cut
Orange prints and solids

For center blocks:
- 72 (1½") squares: 4 dark, 8 medium, 12 light/medium, 16 solid light orange, 20 solid light peach, 12 orange check
- 8 (1" x 1½") orange check rectangles; 8 (1½" x 2") orange check rectangles

For all other blocks:
- 9 (1½"-wide) crosswise strips. Cut strips into 24 (1½"-square) As, 24 (1½" x 2") Ds, 24 (1½" x 3") Es, 24 (1½" x 3½") Hs, and 24 (1½" x 4½") Is.
- 12 (1"-wide) crosswise strips. Cut strips into 24 (1" x 1½") Bs, 24 (1" x 2") Cs, 24 (1" x 3") Fs, 24 (1" x 3½") Gs, 24 (1" x 4½") Js, and 24 (1" x 5") Ks.

Green prints
- 12 (1½"-wide) crosswise strips. Cut strips into 20 (1½"-square) As, 20 (1½" x 2") Ds, 20 (1½" x 3") Es, 20 (1½" x 3½") Hs, 20 (1½" x 4½") Is, 20 (1½" x 5") Ls, and 20 (1½" x 6") Ms.
- 12 (1"-wide) crosswise strips. Cut strips into 24 (1" x 1½") Bs, 24 (1" x 2") Cs, 24 (1" x 3") Fs, 24 (1" x 3½") Gs, 24 (1" x 4½") Js, and 24 (1" x 5") Ks.

Light tan prints
- 9 (1½"-wide) crosswise strips. Cut strips into 16 (1½"-square) As, 16 (1½" x 2") Ds, 16 (1½" x 3") Es, 16 (1½" x 3½") Hs, 16 (1½" x 4½") Is, 16 (1½" x 5") Ls, and 16 (1½" x 6") Ms.
- 8 (1"-wide) crosswise strips. Cut strips into 16 (1" x 1½") Bs, 16 (1" x 2") Cs, 16 (1" x 3") Fs, 16 (1" x 3½") Gs, 16 (1" x 4½") Js, and 16 (1" x 5") Ks.

Orange print for border and outer block rows
- 4 (2½") lengthwise strips. Trim to make 2 (2½" x 44½") border strips and 2 (2½" x 48½") border strips.
- Cut remainder into 9 (1½"-wide) strips. Cut strips into 24 (1½" x 5") Ls and 24 (1½" x 6") Ms.

Quilt Top Assembly
1. For center block (Block 1), lay out 1 dark, 2 medium, 3 light/medium, 4 solid light orange, 5 solid light peach, and 3 orange check squares as shown in *Center Block Diagram*. Add

orange check rectangles and green narrow strips to layout. Join appropriate squares into a strip (*Center Block Assembly Diagram*) and proceed with construction as in a regular block. Make 4 of Block 1.

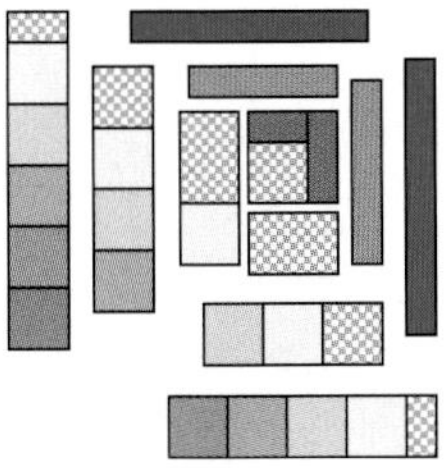

Center Block Assembly Diagram

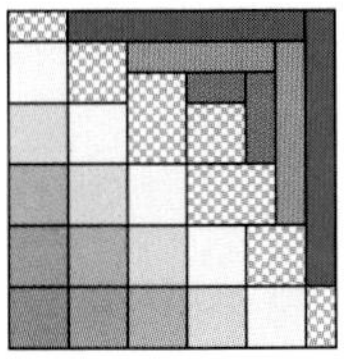

Center Block Diagram
Make 4.

2. Referring to *Block Diagrams*, join appropriate strips in alphabetical order. Make 12 of Block 2, 16 of Block 3, 4 of Block 4, 20 of Block 5, and 8 of Block 6. Note that each block uses 7 different fabrics.

3. Referring to *Quilt Top Assembly Diagram*, lay out blocks as shown. Join into rows; join rows to complete top.

4. Add 1 (2½" x 44½") orange border strip to each side of quilt. Repeat for top and bottom borders.

Quilting

Machine-quilt with a sunburst in center, clamshell fans in each clamshell, and an orange peel in outer border.

Finished Edges

Bind with straight-grain or bias binding made from green print.

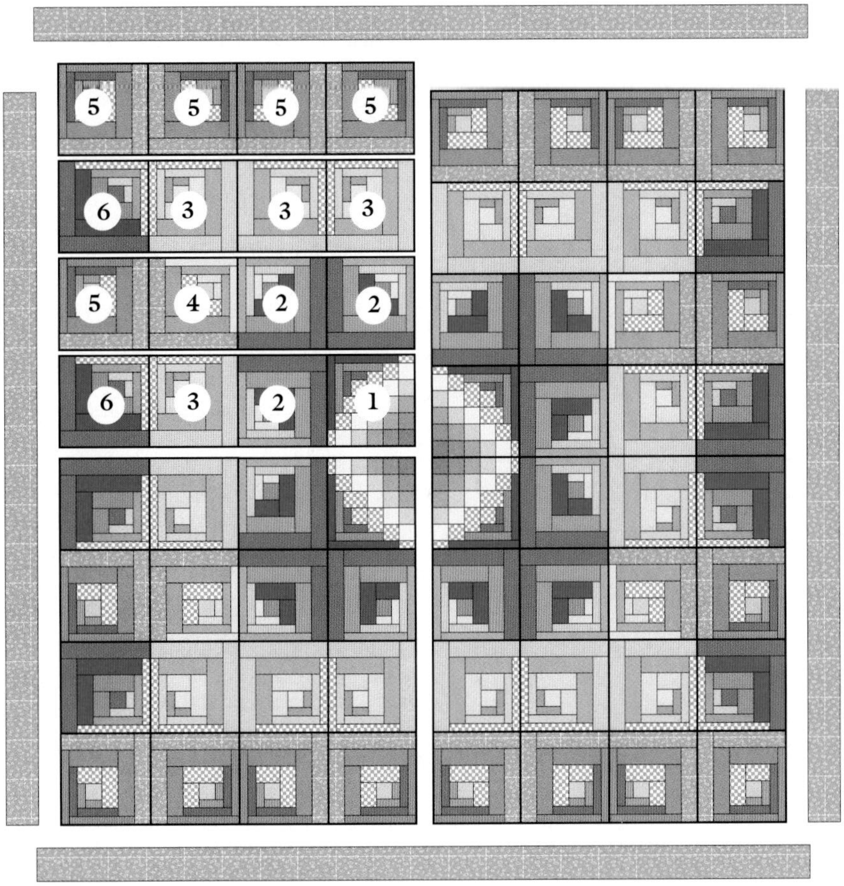

Quilt Top Assembly Diagram

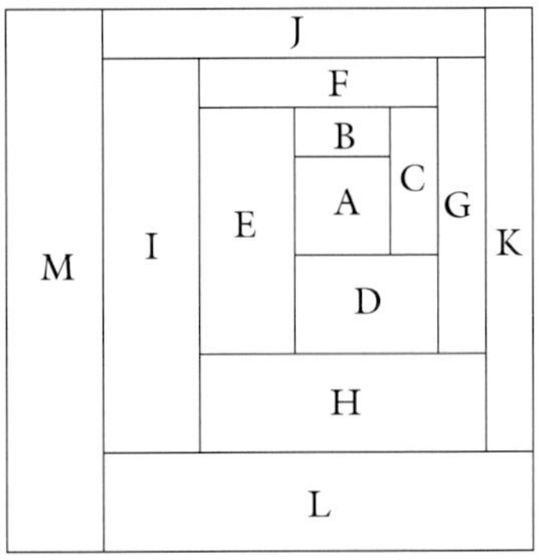

Skeleton Block Diagram

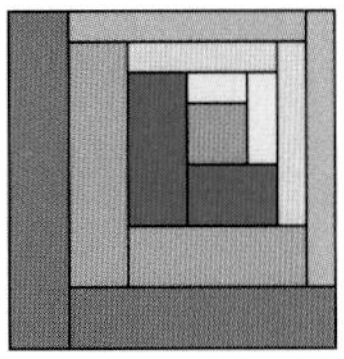

Block 2 Diagram
Make 12.

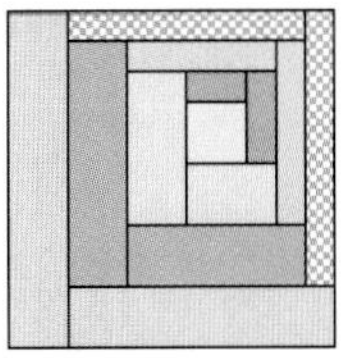

Block 3 Diagram
Make 16.

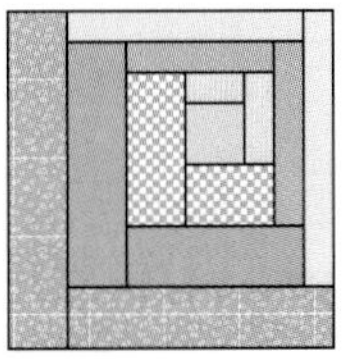

Block 4 Diagram
Make 4.

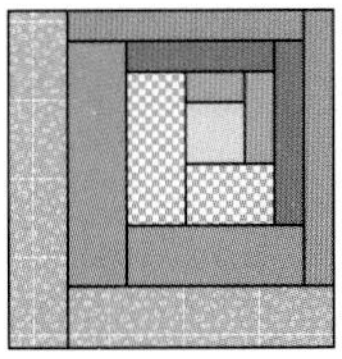

Block 5 Diagram
Make 20.

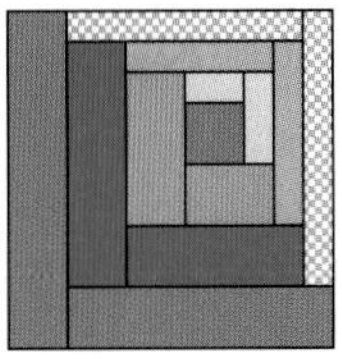

Block 6 Diagram
Make 8.

Eloise Johansen
Macon, Georgia

*E*loise Johansen has always savored memories of growing up during the '30s, watching her grandmother quilt. As a young mother raising five active youngsters, Eloise saved scraps from garment-making, hoping someday she could use them in quilts.

"Quilting has given me a whole new circle of friends."

In 1969, when her last child entered first grade, Eloise finally found time to begin quilting. She didn't know anyone else who quilted and so had to enjoy the activity by herself. The first quilt she made, a Bear's Paw, came from a pattern on a batting wrapper.

"I never did finish quilting it," Eloise recalls. "But I did learn that 180-count percale backing and cotton batting makes for very difficult hand quilting."

Eloise had already made many quilts by the time she started meeting other quilters. In 1985, she was part of a group that formed the Heart of Georgia Quilt Guild in Macon, which is still going strong.

"Quilting has given me a whole new circle of friends," she says, "and my interest has never lagged."

Georgetown Circle
1996

Eloise Johansen says she had no overall plan when she began *Georgetown Circle*. She drafted a pattern, inspired by a picture in a magazine, and started piecing blocks randomly from her scrap bag.

"I went through my accumulation of fabrics and scraps and made one circle at a time," she says, adding that she tried to use fabrics that weren't coordinated. "I did use gold somewhere in each circle.

"I then agonized over my background color," Eloise continues, "limiting myself to something I already had in my stash."

This scrap-bag quilt turned out to be a prize winner. It has been displayed in several shows throughout Georgia. In 1997, it took a blue ribbon for pieced quilts and also the Oxmoor House sponsor's award at the East Cobb guild's show "Georgia Celebrates Quilts," held in Marietta.

Georgetown Circle

Finished Quilt Size
74¼" x 92⅝"

Number of Blocks and Finished Size
12 blocks   20" x 20"

Fabric Requirements
2 yards total assorted reds for stars

3½ yards total assorted lights for stars and circles

3½ yards total assorted blues and browns for circle points

2¼ yards stripe for border

3½ yards assorted dark prints for inner circles and border

3½ yards assorted medium prints for inner circles and border

6½ yards solid dark blue for setting, border triangles, and binding

5½ yards blue print for backing

Pieces to Cut
Reds
- 12 sets of 8 As and 1 B.

Light prints
- 12 sets of 8 Cs and 32 Fs.

Blues and browns
- 12 sets of 32 Gs.

Dark prints
- 12 sets of 8 Ds.
- 12 sets of 8 Es.

Medium prints
- 12 sets of 8 Ds.
- 12 sets of 8 Es.

From all print fabrics except lights
- 126 border triangles H.

Stripe
- 4 (2"-wide) lengthwise strips for borders.

Solid dark blue
- 1 yard for binding.
- 130 border triangles H.
- 6 (20½"-wide) crosswise strips. Cut strips into 12 (20½") background squares.

Quilt Top Assembly

1. Following *Block Assembly Diagram*, join 8 red As and 8 light Cs into a circle. Appliqué 1 matching red B in center. Assemble and add D and E rings (darks can align or alternate as you prefer in each block) Assemble F/G ring and add to complete block. Make 12 circles (*Georgetown Circle Assembly Diagram*).

2. Center and appliqué 1 circle on each blue square (*Block Diagram*). On back of each block, carefully cut away blue fabric from behind circle, leaving ¼" seam allowance. Trim block to 20½"-wide by 20⅛"-long.

3. Join blocks into 4 horizontal rows of 3 blocks each.

4. Center 1 stripe border on each side of center and stitch. Miter corners.

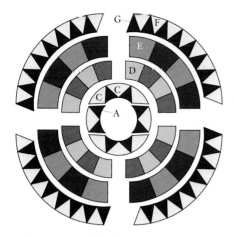

Georgetown Circle
Assembly Diagram

Block Diagram

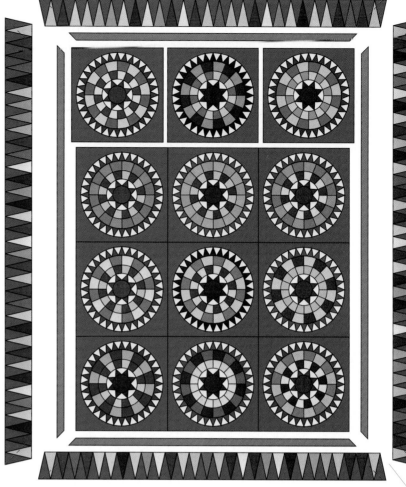

Quilt Top Assembly Diagram

Miter corners.

5. Join solid blue border triangles (H) and print border triangles into a strip as shown in *Border Assembly Diagram*. Make 2 (35 color/36 blue triangle) strips for sides and 2 (28 color/29 blue triangle) strips for top and bottom. Add to quilt. Miter corners, aligning print triangle seams to form corner detail. Outer edge of third triangle should align with inner border.

Quilting

Hand-quilt in-the-ditch around each circle piece, through center of each D and E ring, and through center of each C piece. A feather motif fills blue areas, and

Border Assembly Diagram

stripe border has 2 channels. Pieced border is quilted in-the-ditch and in an opposing triangle pattern.

Finished Edges

Bind with straight-grain or bias binding made from solid blue.

45

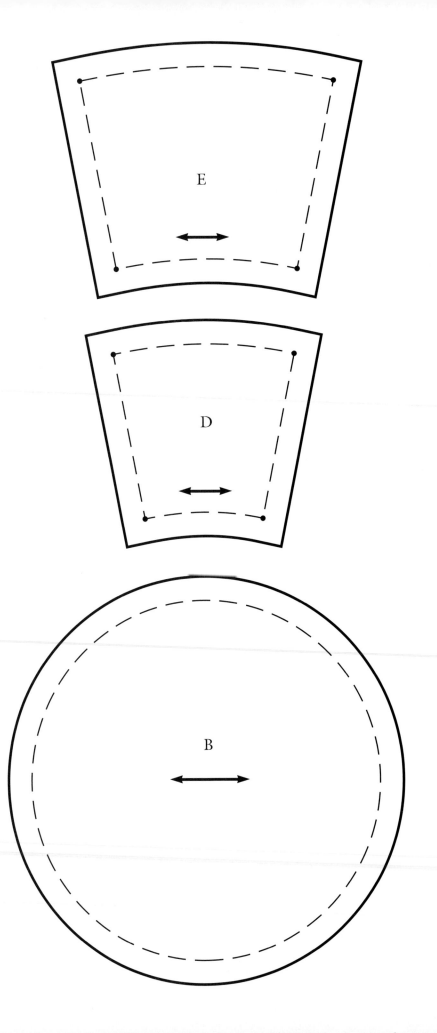

E

D

B

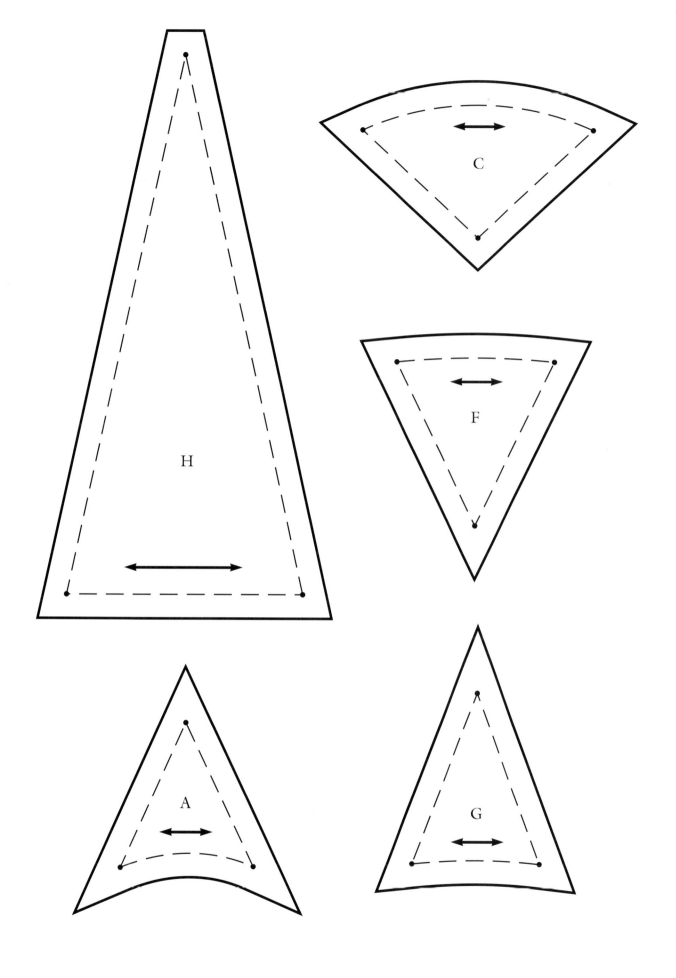

Mabeth H. Oxenreider
Carlisle, Iowa

$\mathcal{M}$abeth H. Oxenreider took a beginner's quilting class in 1980 and was immediately hooked on quilting. "After that, I took any class I could," she says.

"I quilt for myself."

Mabeth likes to make quilts that incorporate a number of techniques: appliqué, piecing, trapunto, etc. She does most of her work on the machine. Mabeth says it's hard to pick a favorite step in the quilting process, but she knows which one she likes least. "I love every step except when I have to mark a whole top," she says.

Mabeth teaches beginner's quilting classes at her local quilt shop, The Quilt Block. "I like to share what I know," she says. "It's really great to see people develop their skills."

Mabeth says she picks projects strictly to please herself. Her work has been juried into the AQS (American Quilter's Society) show in Paducah five times—no small accomplishment! She won a second-place award in traditional pieced quilts in Paducah in 1997.

Friendship Garden
1997

This quilt is an example of the outstanding machine work of its designer and maker, Mabeth H. Oxenreider.

"The poppies were machine-appliquéd using Debra Wagner's method," says Mabeth. "The only handwork is in the corners where I closed the binding."

Mabeth has done a lot of work with colorwash, the technique of piecing picture quilts from small squares, giving them the appearance of watercolor art. She believes this technique has helped her better understand color value. "That is the key to a successful project," she says.

Friendship Garden

Finished Quilt Size
80½" x 91½"

Number of Blocks and Finished Size
1 (38½" x 49½") central appliqué panel, 22 (11" x 18¼") border panels, 4 (12¾" x 12¾") corner border panels

Fabric Requirements
3½ yards assorted pink and orange prints for appliqué, border, and binding

2½ yards assorted green prints for appliqué and piping

¼ yard or scraps assorted brown prints for appliqué

6½ yards white for background

6 yards marbled pink for backing

Other Materials
1/16" cording for binding piping

Pieces to Cut
Pink and orange prints
- 32 (4") squares from assorted prints. Cut squares in quarters diagonally to make 128 quarter-square triangles for inner border.
- 8 (2¼") squares. Cut squares in half diagonally to make 16 half-square triangles for inner border corners.
- 1 yard total for binding.
- For border flowers cut:
  - *22 As.
  - *22 Bs.
  - *22 Cs.
  - *22 Ds.
  - *22 Es.
  - *22 Hs.
  - *30 Js (bud).

- For large flowers in center panel, cut:
  - *4 Os.
  - *4 O rev.
  - *4 Ps.
  - *4 P rev.
  - *4 Qs.
  - *4 Q rev.
  - *4 Rs.
  - *4 R rev.
  - *4 Ss.
  - *4 S rev.
  - *4 Vs.
  - *4 V rev.
  - *4 Ws.
  - *4 W rev.
- For fading flowers in center panel, cut:
  - *2 Xs.
  - *2 X rev.
  - *2 Ys.
  - *2 Y rev.

- For small flowers in corners and center panel, cut:
  - *6 BBs.
  - *2 BB rev.
  - *6 CCs.
  - *2 CC rev.
  - *6 DDs.
  - *2 DD rev.
  - *6 EEs.
  - *2 EE rev.
- Green prints
  - ½ yard for piping.
  - 1 yard for bias (appliqué).
  - 30 Is (bud).
  - 30 Ks (bud).
  - 30 Ls (pod).
  - 22 Ns (border leaves).
  - 22 N rev. (border leaves).
  - 4 Zs (faded flower base).
  - 4 AAs (center panel leaves).
  - 4 AA rev. (center panel leaves).
  - 4 FFs (corner border leaves).

- 4 FF rev. (corner border leaves).

Brown prints
- 22 Fs (border flower center).
- 22 Gs (border flower center).
- 26 Ms (pod top).
- 8 Ts (center flower centers).
- 8 Us (center flower centers).

White
- 1 (39" x 50") rectangle for central panel
- 11 (11½"-wide) crosswise strips. Cut strips into 22 (11½" x 18¾") rectangles for side border panels.
- 2 (13¼"-wide) crosswise strips. Cut strips into 4 (13¼") squares for border corner panels.
- 5 (2½"-wide) crosswise strips. Cut strips into 68 (2½") squares for inner border.

Quilt Top Assembly

1. From remaining green prints, make 30½ yards of ¾"-wide bias. Fold and press to make ¼"-wide finished bias.

2. Referring to center of *Quilt Top Assembly Diagram* and *¼ Center Block Diagram*, appliqué pieces to panel.

3. Referring to *Inner Border Assembly Diagram*, use 2½" white squares and assorted pink and orange half- and quarter-square triangles to make 2 (16-square) top and bottom borders and 2 (18-square) side borders. Add to quilt.

Quilt Top Assembly Diagram

Inner Border Assembly Diagram

4. Referring to *Border Block Diagram* and *Corner Block Diagram*, appliqué pieces as

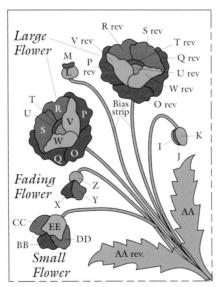

¼ Center Block Diagram

shown. Make 22 border blocks and 4 corner blocks.

5. Join border blocks into 2 (5-block) strips and 2 (6-block) strips). Add to sides of quilt.

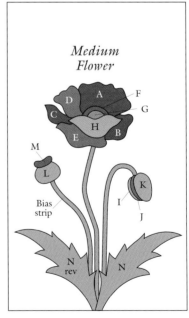

Border Block Diagram

Miter corners of border blocks and set-in corner appliqué blocks.

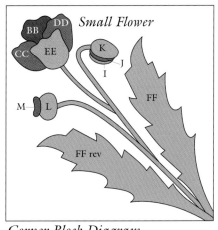

Corner Block Diagram

Quilting

Machine-appliqué and machine-quilt. Quilting is very elaborate. Center panel is outline-quilted around appliqué, and has 4 small motifs between panels. Background is filled with grid quilting. Inner border is grid-quilted in light squares and out-line-quilted around triangles. Outer border is outline-quilted around appliqué, with a circle, swag, and stripe pattern around

each poppy. Outer edges are grid-quilted. Inner border is sur-rounded by poem below, and letter background is closely stip-ple quilted.

Poem from inner border:
FRIENDSHIP GARDEN (top)
FAIREST FLOWER IN GAR-
DEN OF LIFE (left)
IS FELLOWSHIP OF
FRIENDS (bottom)
WITH A FRAGRANCE
THAT NEVER ENDS (right)

Finished Edges

Make piping; add to quilt. Bind with straight-grain or bias bind-ing made with assorted pink prints.

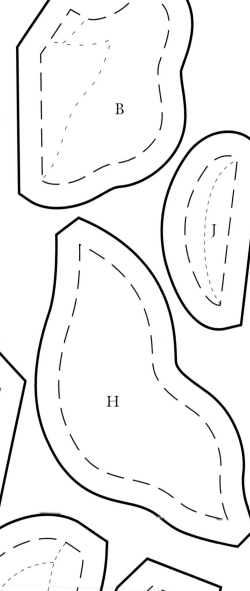

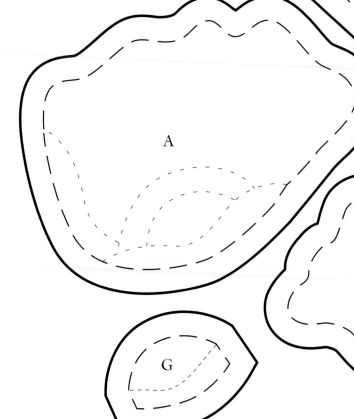

52

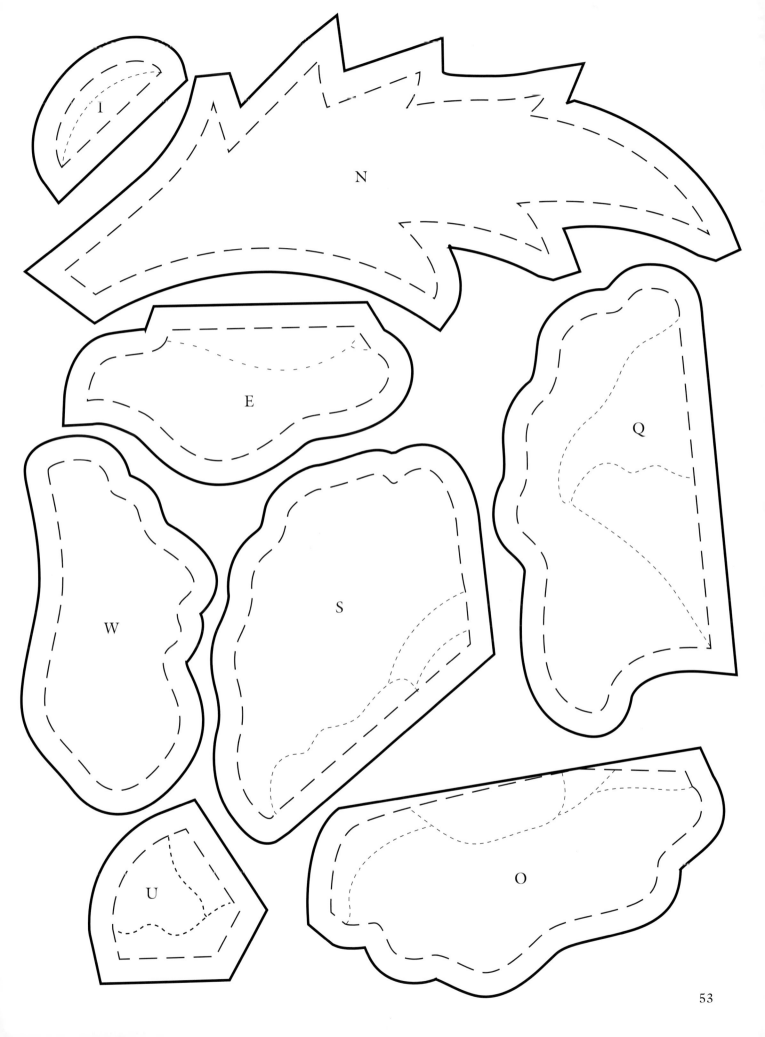

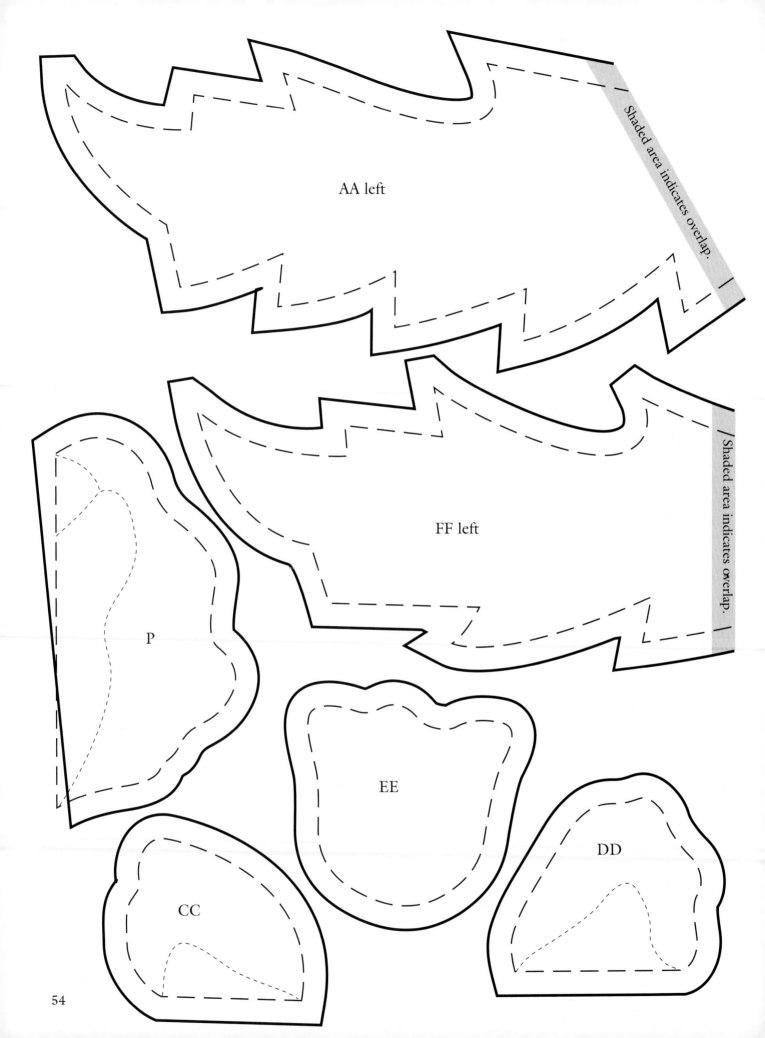

AA left

Shaded area indicates overlap.

Shaded area indicates overlap.

FF left

P

EE

DD

CC

54

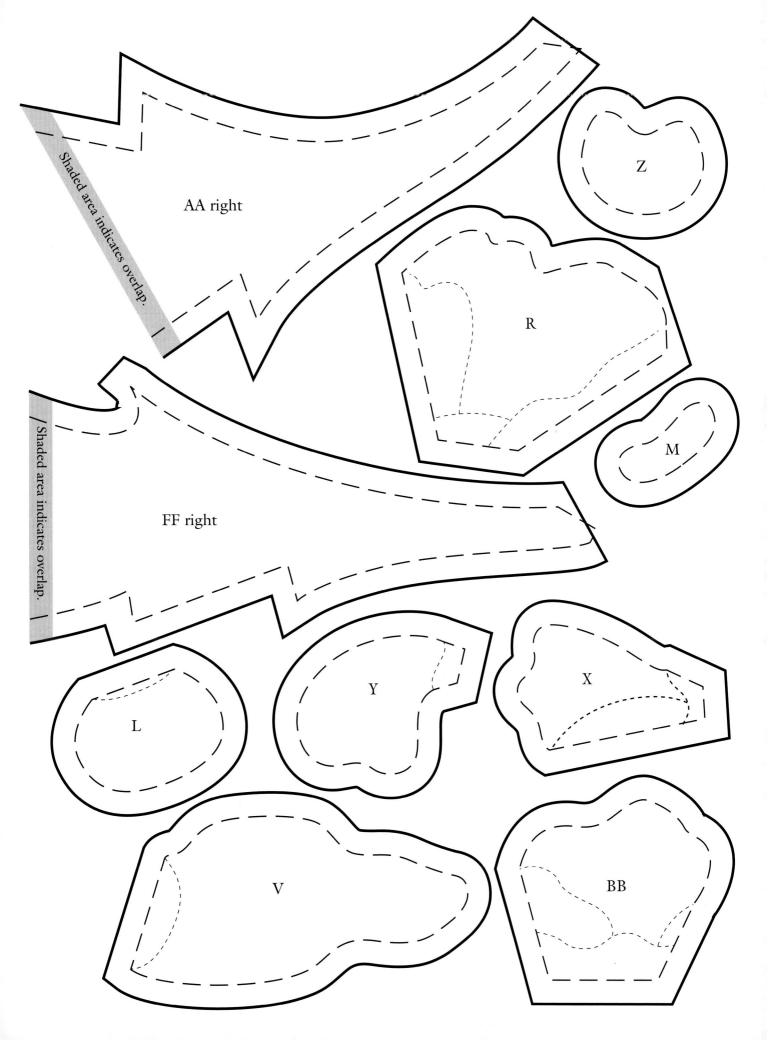

Shaded area indicates overlap.

AA right

Z

Shaded area indicates overlap.

FF right

R

M

L

Y

X

V

BB

Elsie M. Campbell
Arkansas City, Kansas

Growing up, Elsie Campbell learned quilting from her Mennonite mother. But she has been a serious quilter for only about 10 years. Of quilting, she says, "It is who I have become in the past few years."

" I dearly love the hand-quilting process because I can do it anywhere."

Teaching also takes up a big part of Elsie's life. She not only teaches special education classes for gifted children, but is also often asked to teach quilt classes and conduct programs on quilting.

"My family is very supportive," she says. "My husband cooks and does dishes." Elsie's two sons are big helps as well. Kerry accompanies her on road trips, including one to the AQS (American Quilter's Society) show in Paducah, Kentucky. And Kelly is her computer adviser. Both young men are well-compensated for their help. "They both have many quilts," says their mother.

Elsie loves hand quilting because it's portable and she can take it with her to school and on trips. That makes it easier for this busy quilter to keep up with her projects.

"Nearly all of my quilts are traditional pieced with some appliqué details," says Elsie. "I prefer unique interpretations of traditional designs."

Tulip Garden Wedding
1994

This beautiful quilt was born out of a college course on quilting that Elsie Campbell taught at a community college.

"Several of the students requested a special session in construction of a Double Wedding Ring," she explains.

Elsie made a four-ring sample as a teaching aid for the class. She liked it so much that she decided to make a full-size quilt. A friend had asked Elsie to make a quilt with red tulips that he could give to his wife. So Elsie added tulips to the quilt, making it a memorable anniversary gift for her friend's wife.

Elsie credits Shar Jorgansen's "10 rules for quilt design" for helping her with her original adaptation of this traditional quilt pattern. The large white triangular areas in each corner showcase some of Elsie's original quilting designs.

Tulip Garden Wedding

Finished Quilt Size
84" x 84"

Number of Blocks and Finished Size
88 partial rings   4½" x 10"

Fabric Requirements
3½ yards assorted solids (at least 20) for arcs

½ yard each dark red, medium red, and dark green for appliqué

5½ yards mint green for arc centers, connectors, border, and binding

5½ yards white for arc centers, connectors, border, and piping

5 yards white for backing

Other Materials
10 yards ¹⁄₁₆"-diameter soft cording for piping

Stuffing

Pieces to Cut
Assorted solids
- 184 As.
- 176 Bs.
- 176 B rev.
- 252 Cs.
- 252 C rev.

Dark green
- 76 Ds.
- 25 Es (5 Es, 16 ½Es, 4 ¼Es).

Dark red
- 56 Fs.

Medium red
- 56 Gs.

White
- 2½ yards. Cut 4 (8"-wide) lengthwise border strips for appliqué. Use remainder for part of backing.

- 40 Xs.
- 9 Ys.
- 2 (31¾") squares. Cut squares in half diagonally to make 4 half-square triangles for Zs.
- 9 (1"-wide) crosswise strips. Piece to make 10 yards of piping. Insert cording and stitch.

Mint green
- 2½ yards. Cut 4 (6½"-wide) lengthwise outer border strips.
- 1 yard for binding.
- 48 Xs.
- 16 Ys.

Quilt Top Assembly
1. Referring to *Partial Ring Assembly Diagram*, join B rev., 2 C revs., 2 Cs, B, and A into an arc. Join A, B, 2 Cs, 2 C revs., and B rev. into a second arc. Join X to 1 arc, and then add remaining arc to complete partial ring (*Partial Ring*

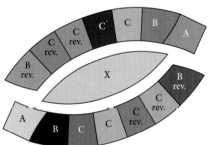

Partial Ring Assembly Diagram

Partial Ring Diagram

Diagram). Make 40 partial rings with white Xs and 48 partial rings with green Xs, varying colors in arcs as desired.

2. To make 4-tulip appliqué blocks, appliqué 4 Ds, 1 full E,

4 Fs, and 4 Gs onto a white Y. Repeat for 5 blocks.

3. Lay out partial rings, 4-tulip appliqué blocks, remaining Ys, and 4 Zs as shown in *Quilt Top Assembly Diagram*. Working from center out, join segments into circles and add Ys. Before adding Z sections, add 8 As to center unit as shown. Join outer segments surrounding each Z, and appliqué arcs to Z, using *Z Diagram* as a placement guide.

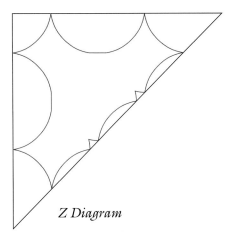

Z Diagram

4. Referring to *Quilt Smart* on page 60, join 4 white border strips into a window, mitering corners. Center quilt over window border. Appliqué outer edges of circle segments to white border. (Y template can be used as a guide here.) Carefully trim excess from back.

5. Appliqué 3 Ds, ½ E, 2 Fs, and 2 Gs in each 2-tulip border section. Appliqué 2 Ds, ¼ E, 1 F, and 1 G in each corner 1-tulip border section.

6. Center 1 green border on each side and stitch to quilt, mitering corners.

Quilt Top Assembly Diagram

White window border

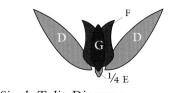

Single Tulip Diagram

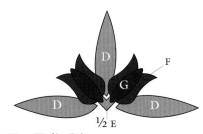

Two-Tulip Diagram

Four-Tulip Diagram

Quilting

Quilt as desired.

Finished Edges

With raw edges aligned, stitch piping to outer edge of quilt. Bind with straight-grain or bias binding made from mint green.

❖ QUILT ❖ SMART

Making Window Border

1. Layer 2 strips, right sides facing. Starting at corner as shown on diagram below, stitch at a 45° angle to end of border strip. Trim.

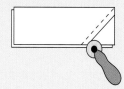

2. Unfold and press. Repeat with 2 remaining strips.

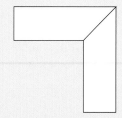

3. Layer 2 sections, right sides facing. Stitch diagonally as shown and trim.

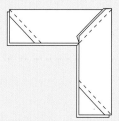

4. Unfold to make window border. Press.

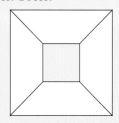

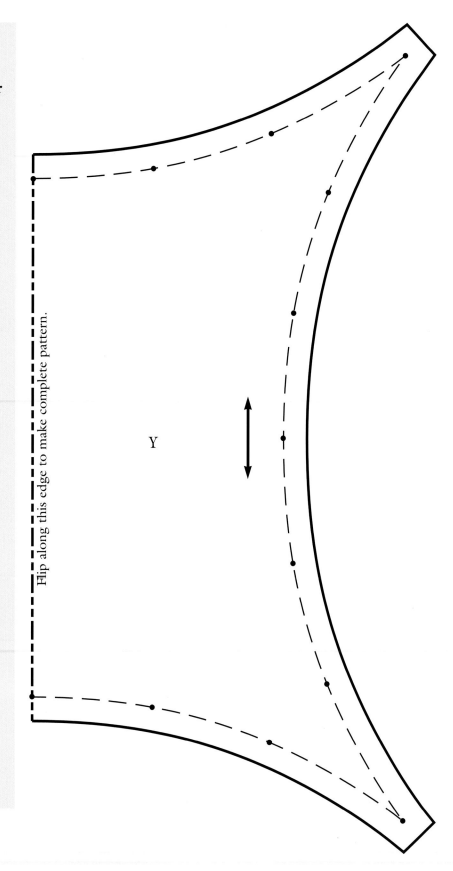

Y

Flip along this edge to make complete pattern.

Evelyn Hunt
Portland, Oregon

I have always enjoyed working with fabric and color," says Evelyn Hunt. "I sewed clothing for my children and grandchildren for many years. But that all came to a stop when I discovered quilts and quiltmaking!"

"For me, quilts and family history are closely related."

Evelyn finds that quilting goes hand-in-hand with her other avid interest—genealogy. When she isn't quilting, traveling, or doing both, this retired teacher-turned-quilter is often researching her family history.

"For me, quilts and family history are closely related," she says. The first quilt Evelyn made was copied from a tattered quilt that had belonged to her grandmother and probably dated before the Civil War.

Evelyn's husband, Jim, is also retired. Together they have plenty of time to explore their shared interests. "I'm fortunate to have the full support of my husband," says Evelyn. She adds that Jim is the source of many great quilting ideas. He has become somewhat of an expert on fabric, techniques, and workmanship.

"We combine our interest in quilting and genealogy with many other interests," says Evelyn, "such as golf, bridge, and just meandering down the road."

Bold Journey
1995

"In the past, when I selected fabrics for a quilt, I found myself eyeing black-and-white prints," says Evelyn Hunt. "But black-and-white prints didn't fit into my traditional quiltmaking."

Evelyn admits she prefers traditional quilt patterns to contemporary designs. When she began making wedding quilts for each of her 15 grandchildren, she dubbed them her Old-fashioned Grandmother Series.

"But after eight traditional wedding quilts," she says, "I was ready for a change. It was time for a 'bold journey.'"

Evelyn drew inspiration and ideas from Michael James's *The Second*

Quiltmaker's Handbook. Using the black-and-white prints she had always been drawn to, she made *Bold Journey* for a grandson who has great appreciation for abstract design. "My husband and I love this quilt," she says, "and we know it will be loved by the young man who receives it."

Bold Journey

Finished Quilt Size
90¼" x 108"

Number of Blocks and Finished Size
72 blocks   10" x 10"

Fabric Requirements*
1¼ yards solid black for pieced borders and blocks (2¾ yards for unpieced borders)

1 yard white-with-large black dots for pieced borders and blocks (2½ yards for unpieced borders)

2¾ yards black-with-small white dots print for pieced borders, binding, and blocks (4¼ yards for unpieced borders)

8½ yards black-and-white print for backing [3 (2¾-yard) panels for backing, extra for blocks]

1 yard each 5 different black-with-white prints for blocks

1 yard each 6 different white-with-black prints for blocks

½ yard white-on-white print for blocks

*Quilt uses 16 different fabrics.

Pieces to Cut
Solid black
- 9 (2⅜"-wide) crosswise strips. Piece to make 2 (2⅜" x 80½") top and bottom border strips and 2 (2⅜" x 94¼") side border strips. [If you prefer unpieced borders, cut 4 (2⅜"-wide) lengthwise strips from alternate yardage and proceed.]
- Use remainder for block pieces.

White-with-large black dots
- 4 (4⅜"-wide) crosswise strips.

Piece to make 2 (4⅜" x 84¼") top and bottom borders strips. [If you prefer unpieced borders, cut 2 (4⅜"-wide) lengthwise strips from alternate yardage and proceed.]
- Use remainder for block pieces.

Black-with-small white dots
- 10 (3¾"-wide) crosswise strips. Piece to make 2 (3¾" x 84¼") top and bottom borders and 2 (3¾" x 108½") side borders. [If you prefer unpieced borders, cut 2 (3¾"-wide) lengthwise strips from alternate yardage and proceed.]
- 1 yard for binding.
- Use remainder for block pieces.

Black-and-white print
- 8¼ yards for backing
- Use remainder for block pieces.

All black-with-white print and solid black remaining fabric
- Cut 36 each of pieces A, B, C rev., and E; and 72 Cs and Ds. Adjust number and fabrics as needed during block assembly.

All white-with-black print and white-on-white remaining fabric
- Cut 36 each of pieces A, B, C rev., and E; and 72 Cs and Ds. Adjust number and fabrics as needed during block assembly.

Quilt Top Assembly

1. Referring to *Block Assembly Diagram* and *Skeleton Block Diagram*, use 11 different fabrics in each block, varying combinations as shown in photo. Choose pieces in dark/light pairs for each section of block. Bottom D piece can be either black or white, as long as it contrasts with adjoining fabrics. Make 72 blocks.

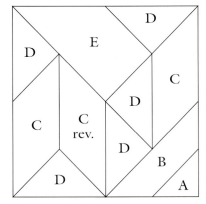

Skeleton Block Diagram

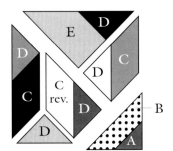

Block Assembly Diagram

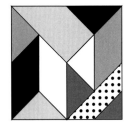

Block Diagram

Quilt Top Assembly Diagram

2. Lay out blocks in 9 horizontal rows of 8 blocks each, as shown in *Quilt Top Assembly Diagram*, rotating top of blocks as shown. Join into rows; join rows to complete center.

3. Add 1 (2⅜" x 80½") black border to top and bottom of quilt. Add remaining black borders to sides.

4. Add 1 (4⅜" x 84¼") white border to top and bottom of quilt.

5. Add 1 (3¾" x 84¼") black dot border to top and bottom of quilt. Add remaining black dot borders to sides.

Quilting

Hand-quilt, using pattern of each fabric as a guide. Dark borders have a zigzag pattern (inner border) or diagonals (outer border).

Finished Edges

Bind with straight-grain or bias binding made from black-with-small white dot print.

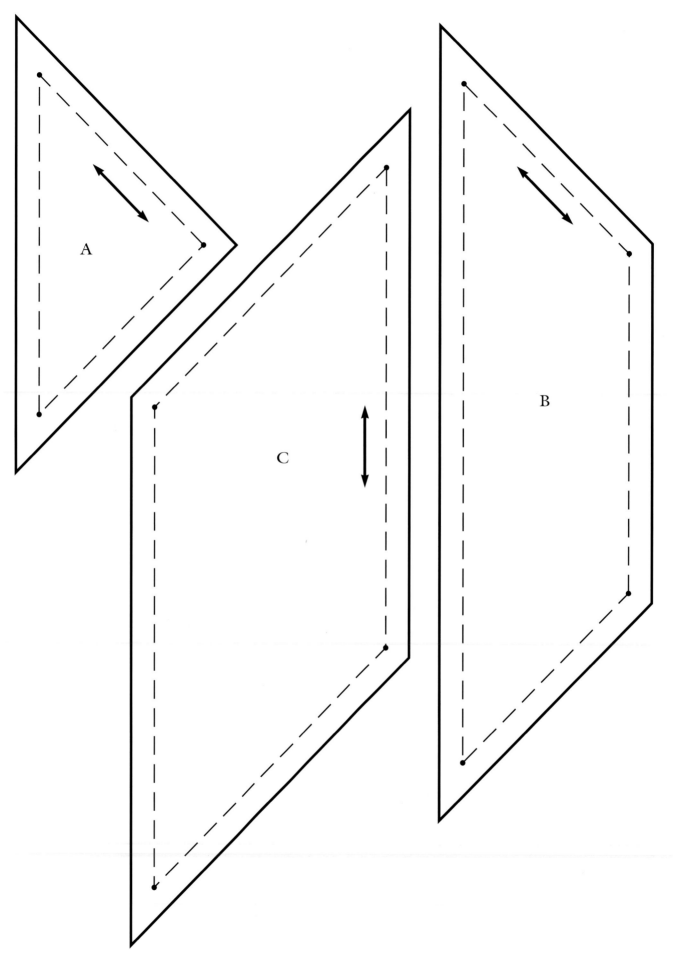

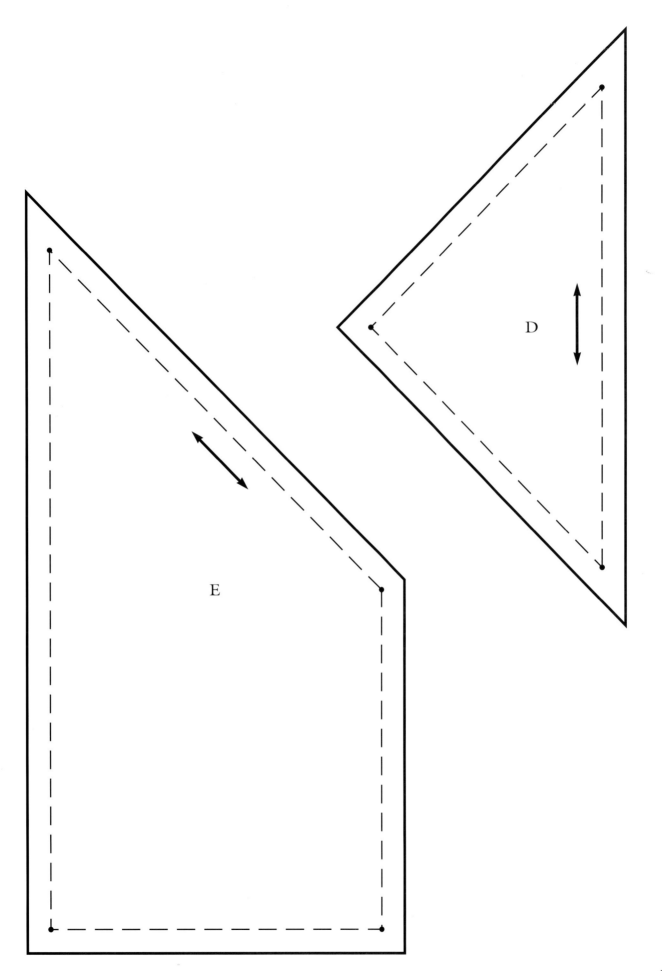

D

E

Traditions in Quilting

Pine Burr

Trumpet Call

Old Thyme
Chain and Star

Nine in the
Window

Plaid Pinwheels

Marion Roach Watchinski
Overland Park, Kansas

*M*arion Roach Watchinski looked forward to her 13th birthday with much anticipation, as do most young girls approaching their teens. But it wasn't the world of make-up, boys, and school dances that she craved. Turning 13 meant she'd be going to junior high where they taught sewing classes.

"I took my first quilting class in the fall of 1983. After that, I educated myself with every quilt book that came on the market."

"Ever since that first sewing class, I've had a continuing love affair with fabric," says Marion.

Marion learned to make her own clothes, which satisfied her fabric fetish for a while. "But starting in college, I had this constant urge to make a quilt.

"I made a feeble attempt," says Marion, "but got discouraged and gave up." Ten years later, she tried again. "I took a class at a local quilt shop and was forever hooked."

By then, Marion was married and had a 3-year-old son. She found that quilting and her choice to be a stay-at-home mom were perfect complements.

"Quilting has provided a wonderful outlet—a way to keep busy and happy when my son was at school or baseball practice or scouts. And yet it let me be there for him when he needed me."

Later, when her son was older, quilting became a way to earn money by working and teaching at a local quilt shop.

Pine Burr
1997

Marion Roach Watchinski loves the look of antique scrap quilts. She also loves well-matched seams and sharp points. When Marion discovered foundation paper piecing, she found the technique she needed to accurately piece some of the intricate antique patterns that had intimidated her in the past.

"At first, I drafted my own patterns and used photocopiers to make my foundations," says Marion. Later, she found a printer who would duplicate her drafted patterns on onion skin, which gave her accurate foundations that were much easier to remove once the block was completed.

Following you'll find patterns and instructions for our quick-piecing method.

Pine Burr

Finished Quilt Size
86" x 98"

Number of Blocks and Finished Size
42 blocks   12" x 12"

Fabric Requirements
5½ yards assorted light prints for blocks (42 fat eighths* or equivalent)

10½ yards assorted dark prints for blocks in rust, blue, green, brown (42 fat quarters** or equivalent)

7½ yards green-with-black print for setting diamonds, borders, border piecing, and binding

8¼ yards fabric for backing [3 (2¾-yard) lengths]

*Fat eighth = 9" x 22" piece

**Fat quarter = 18" x 22" piece

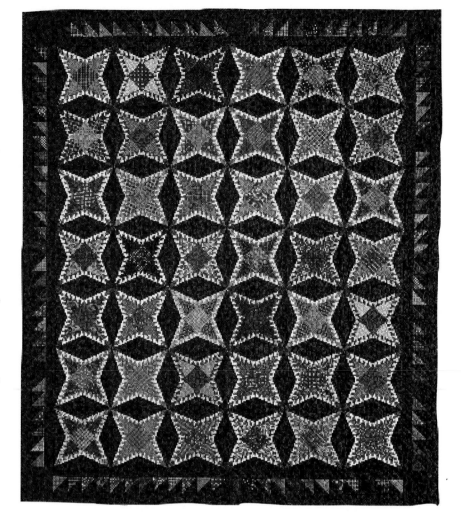

Pieces to Cut
Assorted light prints
- 42 sets of
  *1½ (1⅞" x 44") strips. These will be used to quick-piece A units. [If using fat eighths, cut 3 (1⅞" x 22") strips from each fabric.]
  *4 (1⅞") squares. Cut squares in half diagonally to make 8 light A triangles.

Assorted dark prints
- 42 sets of
  *1½ (1⅞" x 44") strips. These will be used to quick-piece A units. [If using fat quarters, cut 3 (1⅞" x 22") strips from each fabric.]
  *4 Bs.
  *1 D.
- 42 sets of 4 Cs.
- 26 (3⅞" x 7¾") F rectangles

Green-with-black print
- 16 (2½"-wide) crosswise strips. Piece to make 4 (2½" x 84½") border strips and 4 (2½" x 72½") border strips.
- 1 (7½"-wide) crosswise strip. Cut strip into 4 (7½") squares for border squares.
- 168 Es.
- 6 (3⅞"-wide) crosswise strips. Cut strips into 26 (3⅞" x 7¾") F rectangles.

Block Assembly
Note: Each block has 32 half-square triangle A units, 8 additional light A triangles, 4 B diamonds, 4 Cs, 1 D, and 4 Es. All pieces in a group (i.e., 4 Cs) are the same fabric. In most blocks, dark As, Bs, and D match.

Instructions for matching sets:

1. Choose 1 light and 1 dark 1⅞"-wide strip. Mark light strip with 1⅞" squares for half-square triangles (See *Quilt Smart*, page 11). Match strips, stitch, cut, and press. Make 32 half-square triangle A units for each block.

2. Join 4 A units into a strip. Make 8 strips, orienting as shown in *Block Quadrant Diagram*. Add 1 light A to end of each strip.

3. Referring to *Block Quadrant Diagram*, add 1 A strip to side of 1 C. Add 1 B to 1 A strip. Add A/B strip to opposite side of C to make 1 block quadrant. Make 4 matching quadrants.

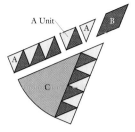

Block Quadrant Diagram

4. Join quadrants with D. Add Es to complete block, as shown in *Pine Burr Block Diagram.*

5. Make 42 blocks.

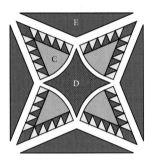

Pine Burr Block Assembly Diagram

Pine Burr Block Diagram

Quilt Top Assembly

1. Lay out blocks in 7 horizontal rows of 6 blocks each as shown in *Quilt Top Assembly Diagram.*

2. Join rows to complete top.

3. Choose 1 green and 1 dark 3⅞" x 7¾" rectangle. Mark for 3⅞" half-square triangles as before. Stitch, cut, and press. Repeat to make 104 F units.

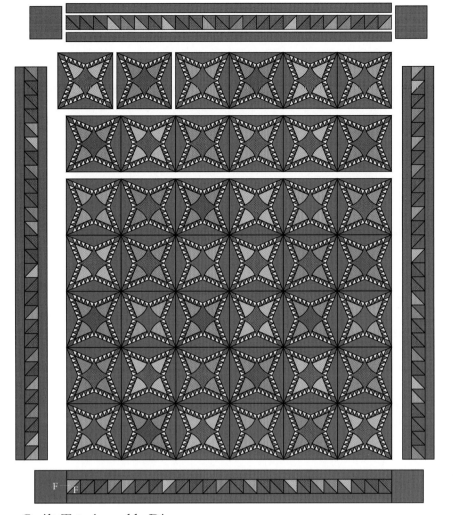

Quilt Top Assembly Diagram

4. Join 24 F units into a strip as shown in *Quilt Top Assembly Diagram.* Make 2 (24-unit) strips and 2 (28-unit) strips, turning units as shown.

5. Join 1 (2½") green border strip to each side of corresponding F unit strip. Repeat for 4 strips.

6. Add 1 (28-unit) strip set to sides of quilt. Add 1 (7½") green square to each end of remaining strips. Add to top and bottom of quilt.

Quilting

Quilt concentric circles centered on each block intersection. Quilt border in diagonal rows.

Finished Edges

Bind with straight-grain or bias binding made from green-with-black print.

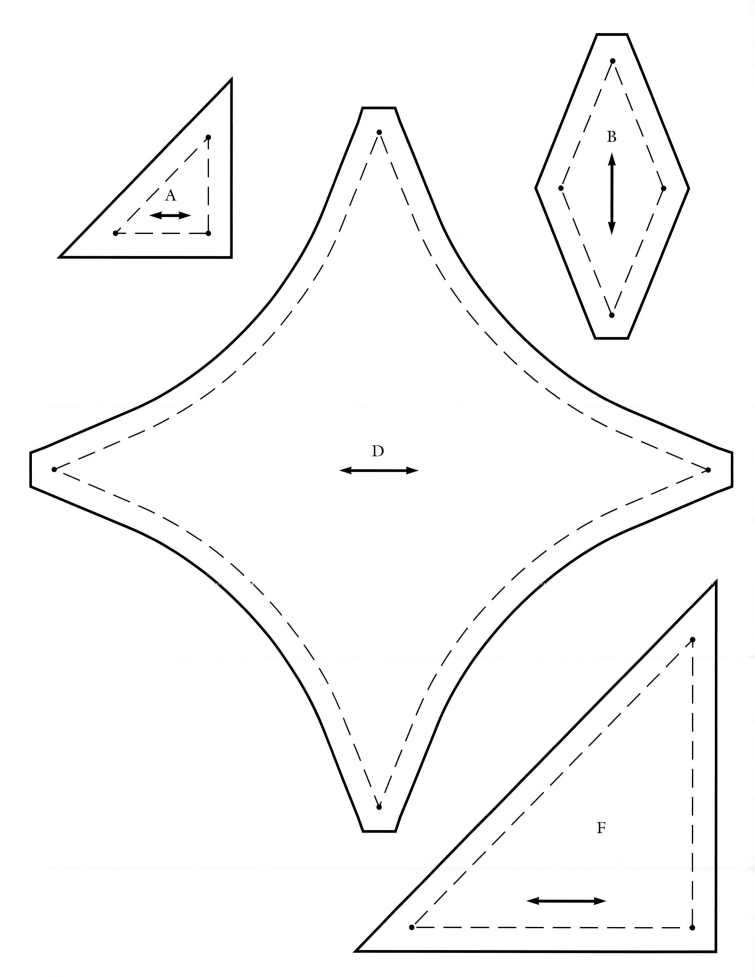

A

B

D

F

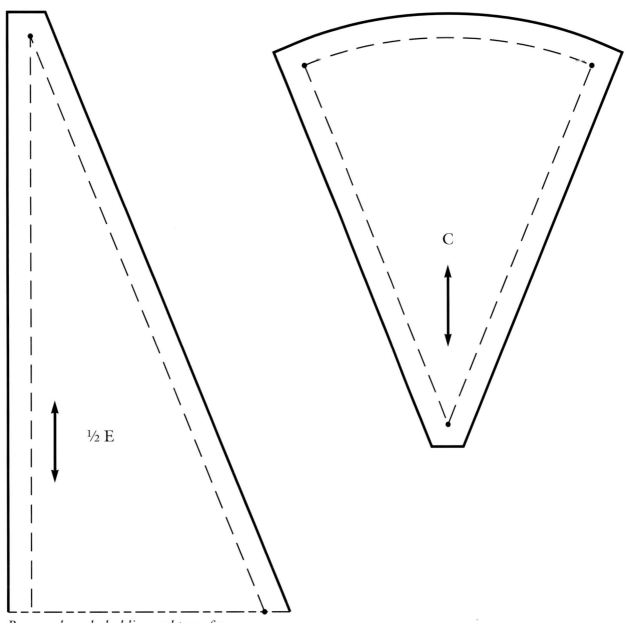

½ E

Reverse along dashed line and trace for
complete pattern E.

C

Jennifer Suter
Kennesaw, Georgia

*J*ennifer Suter had never made a quilt until about eight years ago. "One day, while on my way to a restaurant, I passed Tiny Stitches, a quilt shop in nearby Marietta," she recalls.

Something in the shop's window caught Jennifer's interest (she's not sure just what). She went back the next day and signed up for an eight-week-long beginner's class.

"My Christian faith is very important to me," says Jennifer. *"I put a Bible verse on each one of my hand-made quilt labels."*

Jennifer's first love is appliqué. "I love appliqué quilts above all others and have one in the works at all times," she says.

She finds inspiration for her quilt designs in all kinds of places: magazines, china, rugs, nature, and especially in the Bible.

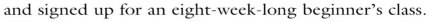

Trumpet Call
1997

This quilt is Jennifer Suter's version of red-and-green appliqué, a quilt style that was popular during the mid-1800s. "My inspiration was a picture in a magazine of a museum quilt from the 1860s," says Jennifer.

The habit of placing an intentional mistake in a quilt as a "gift to God" is also a 19th-century tradition. And Jennifer followed this tradition when making her quilt. *Trumpet Call* contains 561 appliquéd red circles and 39 green ones. She intentionally made one green circle red.

Jennifer's quilt took a third-place ribbon in Large Traditional Appliqué in the East Cobb Quilters' Guild Quilt Show in Marietta in 1997.

Trumpet Call

Finished Quilt Size
81" x 81"

Fabric Requirements
3½ yards dark green print for appliqué

1 yard green solid for appliqué

4 yards dark red print for appliqué

2¼ yards light red print for appliqué

⅛ yard red solid for appliqué

7½ yards cream print for background and borders

5 yards fabric for backing

1 yard dark red print for binding

Pieces to Cut
Dark green print
- 40 Ds.
- 20 Fs.
- 80 Hs.
- 16 Is.
- 16 Os.
- 4 Ps.

Dark red print
- 5 As.
- 5 Cs.
- 560 Ds.
- 20 Es.
- 280 Gs.
- 16 Js.
- 16 Ls.
- 4 Qs.

Light red print
- 5 Bs.
- 5 Ds.
- 16 Ks.
- 16 Ns.
- 4 Rs.

Red solid
- 16 Ms.

Cream print
- 5 (16½"-wide) crosswise strips. Cut strips into 9 (16½") squares for center blocks.
- 1 (2½-yard) length. Cut lengthwise into 3 (14" x 84") outer border strips.
- 1 (2½-yard) length. Cut lengthwise into 1 (14" x 84") outer border strip and 4 (3½" x 57") inner border strips.

Quilt Top Assembly
1. From green solid, make 700" of ¾"-wide bias. Fold and press to make ¼"-wide finished bias. If shorter sections are easier for you to work with, make 70 (10") sections of bias.

2. Fold 1 (16½") cream print square into quarters and crease to make appliqué placement guidelines. Referring to *Appliqué Block Placement Diagram*, appliqué pieces A–H as shown onto 1 (16½") cream print square. (See *Quilt Smart* on page 80 for tips on appliquéing small circles.) Make 5 blocks.

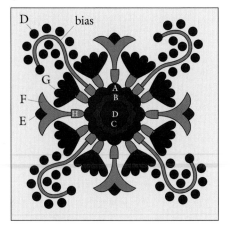

Appliqué Block Placement Diagram

3. Join 5 appliqué blocks and 4 plain blocks as shown in *Quilt Top Assembly Diagram* to make quilt center.

4. Join 3½" x 57" cream borders to quilt, mitering corners.

5. Join 14" x 84" cream borders to quilt, mitering corners.

6. Referring to *Border* and *Corner Appliqué Placement Diagrams* and to *Quilt Top Assembly Diagram*, appliqué borders and corners as shown. Borders may be appliquéd before adding to quilt top, but corner work must be done after joining to quilt.

Quilt Top Assembly Diagram

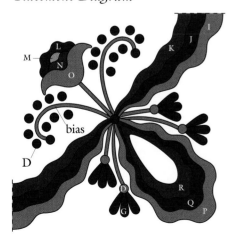

Border Appliqué Placement Diagram

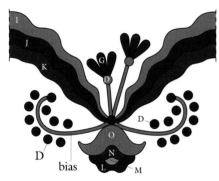

Corner Appliqué Placement Diagram

Quilting

Outline-quilt around appliqué in each block. Quilt appliqué pattern in plain blocks. Quilt 3" border using Bud Quilting Pattern (page 84). Outline-quilt around appliqué in border, and fill background with a stripe pattern.

Finished Edges

Bind with straight-grain or bias binding made from dark red print.

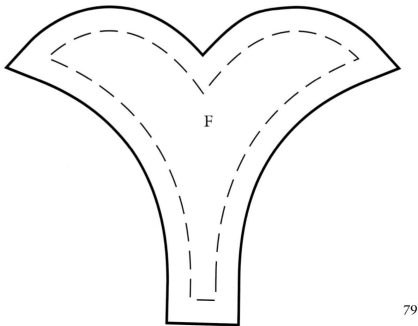

79

❖QUILT SMART❖
Appliquéing Small Circles

Small circles can be difficult to appliqué. Sometimes in the stitching, they cease to be circles and turn into unsightly lumps. Follow these steps for easy successful small-circle appliqué:

1. Trace circle pattern D (*without* seam allowance) onto freezer paper. Trace a separate circle for each piece needed. Cut out circles on drawn lines.

2. Use template to trace circles on the wrong side of your fabric. Again, trace as many circles as you will need for your quilt. Cut out circles, adding ¼" seam allowance.

3. Run a basting stitch around each fabric circle, sewing halfway between drawn line and cut edge as shown in *Diagram 1.* Keep needle and thread attached.

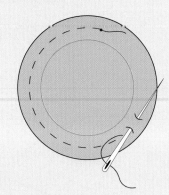

Diagram 1

4. Place paper template on center of wrong side of fabric circle and pull basting thread to gather fabric over paper template as shown in *Diagram 2.* When fabric is tight, space gathers evenly and make backstitch or knot to secure thread. Cut thread. Repeat for all fabric circles.

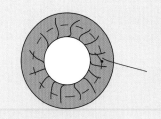

Diagram 2

5. Pin circle in place and appliqué.

6. Carefully trim a circle of fabric from behind the appliqué circle, leaving ¼" seam allowance and exposing the paper template. Pull paper template out through the hole as shown in *Diagram 3.* Remove basting stitches. Discard paper template.

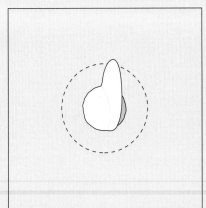

Diagram 3

Reverse along dashed line and trace for complete pattern piece R.

G

½ R

E

Darlene K. Orton
Salina, Kansas

*D*arlene Orton has been sewing clothes since age 10, but she didn't start making quilts until 1980, when she took a sampler quilt class.

"The best part of a new project is the excitement of choosing the fabric and pattern. The second best part is making the label for the finished quilt."

"I made my first five quilts by hand," she says. "Then I found out that machine piecing was acceptable, and I haven't stopped since."

Darlene and her husband, who retired in 1997, spend seven months of each year traveling in their motor home.

"I take my Pfaff sewing machine and several projects with me so I can keep busy," says Darlene.

When she's not traveling, Darlene spends time with her five children and 11 grandchildren. She and her four daughters have lots in common, since they're quilters, too.

"My oldest daughter and I attend the American Quilter's Society show in Paducah each year," says Darlene.

Old Thyme Chain and Star
1995

"I loved this quilt from the first time I saw it in the New Jersey quilt book," says Darlene Orton. She's talking about *New Jersey Quilts*, published in 1992 by the Heritage Quilt Project of New Jersey. The quilt Darlene loved so had been made in the 1840s and was part of New Jersey's quilt documentation project.

Darlene wanted to make her own version of the quilt, but she wanted to stay true to the colors and fabrics of the period.

"The patterns were easy," says Darlene. "The challenging part was gathering enough of the right fabrics." Being a self-described fabricholic, Darlene says that was also the fun part.

Old Thyme Chain and Star

Finished Quilt Size
106½" x 121½"

Number of Blocks and Finished Size
98 star blocks   7½" x 7½"
97 (25-patch) blocks 7½" x 7½"

Fabric Requirements
8½ yards total assorted prints and plaids (red, pink, brown, blue)
7½ yards muslin
1½ yards red print for swags
½ yard red solid for appliqué stars and bows
10 yards fabric for backing and binding

Other Materials
Red embroidery thread

Pieces to Cut
Assorted prints and plaids
- 97 matching sets of 4 (2") squares (A).
- 97 matching sets of 8 (2") squares (B).
- 97 matching sets of 4 (2") squares (C).
- 97 matching sets of 4 (2") squares (D).
- 97 (2") squares (E).
- 98 matching sets of 3 (2¾") squares. Cut squares in quarters diagonally to make 12 quarter-square triangles for star points (G).
- 98 (2") squares matching G triangles for star centers (H).
- 98 matching sets of 4 (2") squares for star corners (I).

Muslin
- Cut 3½ yards. From this, cut 4 (5"-wide) lengthwise strips for borders.
- Remaining fabric will be approximately 22" wide. From this cut:
  *13 (2¾"-wide) crosswise strips. Cut strips into 98 (2¾") squares. Cut squares in quarters diagonally to make 392 quarter-square triangles for star points (G).
  *45 (2"-wide) crosswise strips. Cut strips into 495 (2") squares (F).
- From full width of muslin, cut 70 (2"-wide) strips. Cut strips into 1,461 additional 2" squares (F). You should have a total of 1,956 squares (F).

Red print for swags
- 22 side swags.
- 18 top/bottom swags.

Red solid
- 36 stars.
- 4 bows (4 each Y, Z).

Backing fabric
- Cut 1 yard and reserve for binding.
- Cut remaining yardage into 3 (3-yard) lengths. Join to make a pieced backing with horizontal seams.

Block Assembly
Star Block

1. Choose a star fabric set (12 Gs and 1 H) and a star corners fabric set (4 Is). Join 2 Gs to make a half-square. Join 1 star G and 1 muslin G to make a half-square. Join to make a star point square as shown in *Star Point Diagram*. Make 4 star point units.

Star Point Diagram

2. Lay out star points and matching star center (H) with 4 corners (I) and 16 muslin squares (F). Join into rows; join rows to complete block as shown in *Star Block Diagram*.

3. Make 98 star blocks.

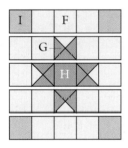

Star Block Assembly Diagram

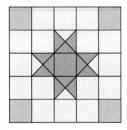

Star Block Diagram

25-Patch Block

1. Choose 1 set each of A, B, C, D, and E fabrics. Lay out with 4 muslin squares (F) as shown in *25-Patch Block Assembly Diagram*.

2. Join into rows; join rows to complete block as shown.

3. Make 97 (25-Patch) blocks.

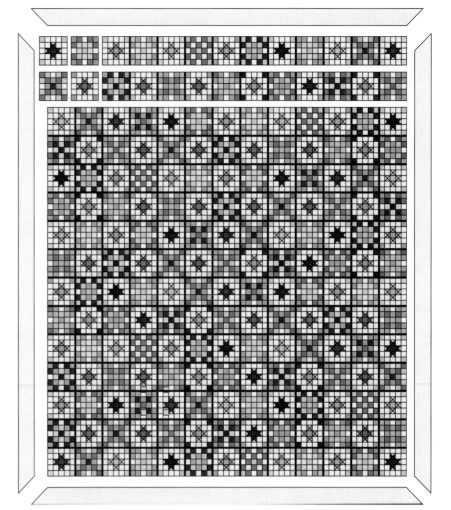

Quilt Top Assembly Diagram

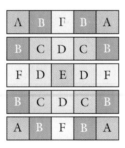

25-Patch Block Assembly Diagram

Quilt Top Assembly

1. Lay out blocks in 15 horizontal rows of 13 blocks each, alternating star blocks and 25-Patch blocks, as shown in *Quilt Top Assembly Diagram*. Join into rows; join rows to complete quilt top.

2. Join 1 border to each side of quilt, centering each strip. Miter corners.

3. Appliqué swags, stars, and bows as shown in photo. Stem-stitch a circle to define bow "knot."

Quilting

Hand-quilt in-the-ditch around each star and around muslin surrounding each star. Quilt diagonally through each chain. Echo-quilt around each swag to fill border.

Finished Edges

Bind with straight-grain or bias binding made from backing print.

88

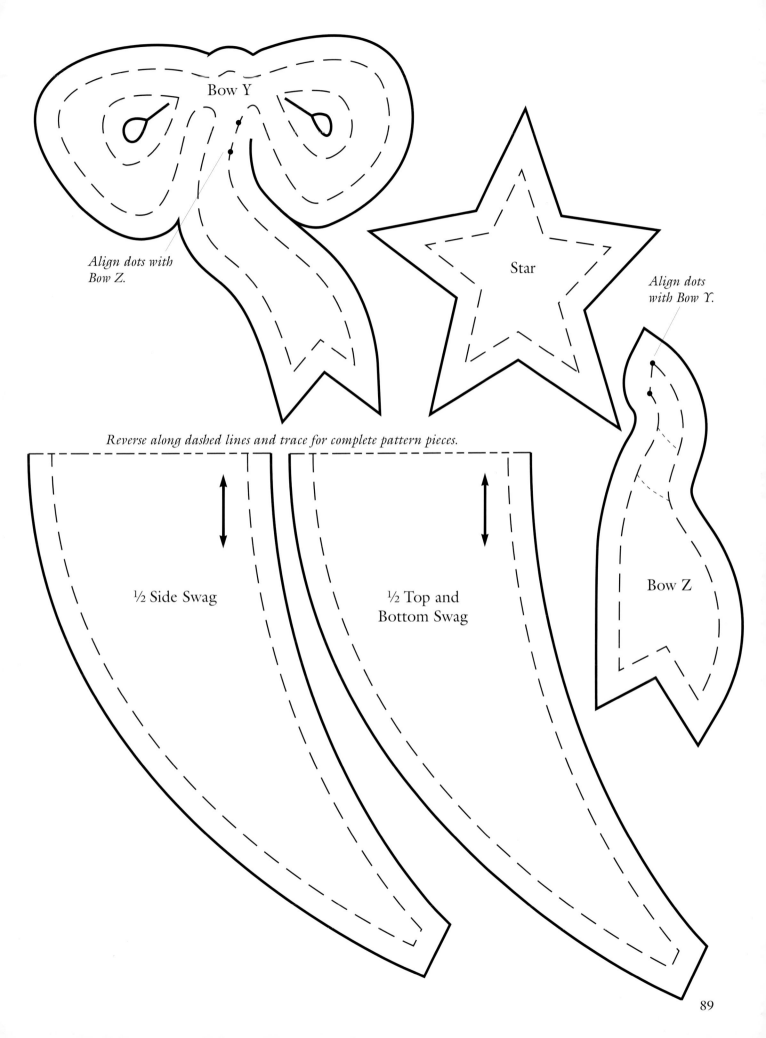

Bow Y

Align dots with Bow Z.

Star

Align dots with Bow Y.

Bow Z

Reverse along dashed lines and trace for complete pattern pieces.

½ Side Swag

½ Top and Bottom Swag

Charlene Bement
Rancho Cucamonga, California

Charlene Bement has been quilting since childhood. "As a child I always liked creating things," she says. "At first it was mud pies and other really big messes." But eventually Charlene moved on to less messy endeavors such as dolls, quilts, and pot holders.

"I've found that there are lots of quilters just like me—with unfinished projects."

Charlene loves hand quilting and designs her own quilt patterns, which she sells though her quilting supply business, Quilters' Haven. She spends a lot of time on the road as a vendor and teacher at quilt shows all over the country.

Charlene says she is always looking for ways to make quilting quicker and easier. "If it's not quick and easy," she says, "I get impatient and don't finish the project. But I've found, over the years, that there are lots of quilters just like me—with unfinished projects. Can you believe it?"

Nine in the Window
1992

"I always loved the old traditional Glorified Nine Patch pattern," say Charlene Bement. "But I wasn't crazy about the idea of sewing all those points."

Charlene admits that she is impatient and likes to develop faster and easier ways to do traditional patterns. A math lover, she says she sketched and sewed and figured and sewed some more until she had discovered a quick method for this quilt design, which is a combination of Nine-patch blocks and Cathedral Windows.

After she made her first *Nine in the Window* in 1992, she got many requests for the pattern. Now she produces and sells the pattern along with a set of plastic templates. You may contact her at:

Charlene Bement
Quilters' Haven
7662 Ramona Avenue
Rancho Cucamonga, CA
91730

Nine in the Window

Finished Quilt Size
69½" x 86"

Number of Blocks and Finished Size
78 blocks   11¾" x 11¾"

Fabric Requirements
¼ yard green print
2 yards white-on-white print
4½ yards light print
12½ yards purple print
King-size batting

Pieces to Cut
Make a 12¼"-diameter circle template using a compass.
Green print
- 3 (2¼"-wide) crosswise strips. Cut strips into 48 (2¼") squares (A).

White-on-white
- 28 (2¼"-wide) crosswise strips. Cut strips into 192 (2¼" x 5½") rectangles (B).

Light print
- 28 (5½"-wide) crosswise strips. Cut strips into 192 (5½") squares (C).

Purple print
- 108 (12¼") circles.

Batting
- 78 (12¼") circles.

Block Assembly
1. Join 1 A, 4 Bs, and 4 Cs as shown in *Nine-Patch*

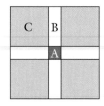

Nine-Patch Diagram

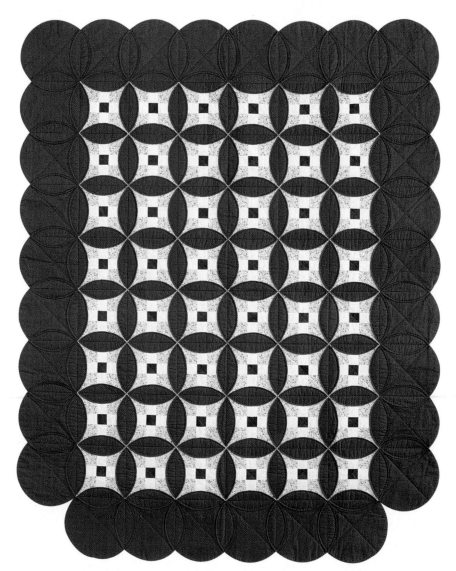

Diagram to make a Nine-Patch. Make 48 blocks.

2. Place 1 block and 1 purple circle together with right sides facing. Place on top of 1 batting circle with purple circle facing up. Stitch ¼" from edge, leaving a 3" opening for turning. Trim excess fabric and clip curves. Turn right side out and press. Slipstitch opening closed. Make 48 nine-patch round blocks.

3. Repeat Step 2 with 2 purple circles to make 30 border blocks.

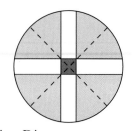

Quilting Diagram

4. Machine-quilt across each block to divide circle in quarters as shown in *Quilting Diagram*.

5. Lay out blocks. Place 2 adjacent blocks together, with back sides facing, and quilting matching. Stitch together between quilted X ends, 1¾"

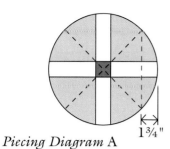

Piecing Diagram A

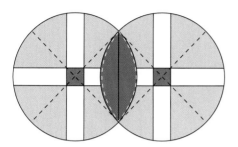

Piecing Diagram B

from circle edge as shown in red in *Piecing Diagram A*. Open blocks and fold down resulting arcs as shown in *Piecing Diagram B*. Machine-quilt edges of arcs in place.

6. Work top to bottom, row by row, to complete quilt as shown in *Quilt Top Assembly Diagram*. Quilted arcs will form interlocking circles. Resulting square blocks will measure 8¼".

Quilting
Since blocks are quilted as they are made, no other quilting is needed.

Finished Edges
Edges are already finished, so no binding is required.

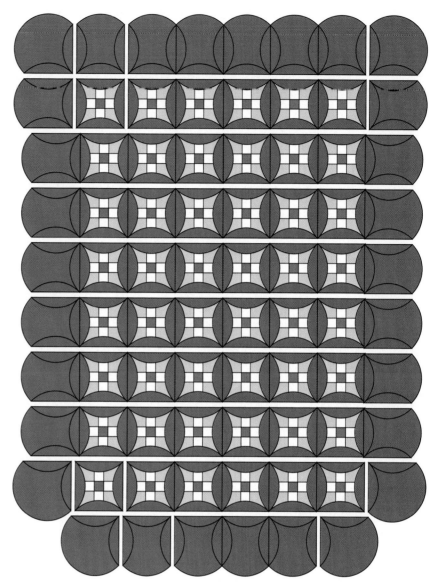

Quilt Top Assembly Diagram

Lila Taylor Scott
Marietta, Georgia

When Lila Taylor Scott's mother passed away, she left two sets of quilt blocks. Lila wanted to turn these precious blocks into quilts, but she'd never made a quilt and didn't know where to start. So she checked out all the quilt books at the library and taught herself the art of quiltmaking.

"I like taking classes and learning all that I can about quilting."

Thus began a hobby that has become more dear to Lila with the passing of each of the 11 years since.

"Quilting has become my main hobby," says Lila. "I belong to a weekly quilting group as well as a guild that meets monthly."

Lila has also turned quilting into a part-time profession, working as a technical writer and editor for quilt instructions.

Plaid Pinwheels
1997

"I like designing my own quilts with traditional patterns," says Lila Scott. "I like to change traditional patterns into quick-pieced ones."

Lila also likes pinwheels—the revolving toy wheel on a stick that spins in the wind. So when she found the pinwheel block in Barbara Brackman's *Encyclopedia of Quilt Patterns*, she decided it was a good starting point for her next quilt.

"I wanted the quilt to show motion," says Lila, "so I did an off-set placement. I also changed the pattern so it could be quick-cut and quick-pieced."

Plaid Pinwheels

Finished Quilt Size
91" x 99"

Number of Blocks and Finished Size
90 blocks   8" x 8"

Fabric Requirements
1½ yards light print for center background

4 yards light print for outer background

5 yards total scraps assorted medium and dark plaids and prints for pinwheels (yellow, pink, red, orange, brown, green, blue, purple)

1½ yards green check for inner border

½ yard red print for border

2¾ yards green print for outer border

1 yard dark green print for binding

9 yards [3 (3-yard) lengths] fabric for backing

Pieces to Cut
Light print for center background
- 6 (2½" wide) crosswise strips. Cut strips into 88 (2½") squares for center Goose Chase units.
- 13 (2½"-wide) crosswise strips. Cut strips into 112 (2½" x 4½") rectangles for center background and spacer units.

Light print for outer background
- 17 (2½"-wide) crosswise strips. Cut strips into 272 (2½") squares for outer Goose Chase units.

- 31 (2½"-wide) crosswise strips. Cut strips into 272 (2½" x 4½") rectangles for outer background.
- 1 (8½"-wide) crosswise strip. Cut strip into 4 (8½") squares for spacers.
- 1 (4½"-wide) crosswise strip. Cut strip into 4 (4½" x 8½") rectangles for spacers.

Assorted medium and dark plaids and prints for pinwheels
- 90 sets of 4 (2½") squares.
- 90 sets of 4 (2½" x 4½") rectangles.

Green check for inner border
- 4 (4½"-wide) lengthwise strips.

Red print for border
- 9 (1½"-wide) crosswise strips. Piece to make 2 (1½" x 88½") side border strips and 2 (1½" x 82½") top and bottom border strips.

Green print for outer border
- 4 (5"-wide) lengthwise strips. Cut 2 (5" x 90½") side border strips and 2 (5" x 91½") top and bottom border strips.

Quilt Top Assembly
1. Using diagonal-seams method and referring to *Diagonal Seams Diagrams*, make a Goose Chase unit using 1 (2½" x 4½") medium or dark rectangle, 1 (2½") medium or dark square, and 1 (2½") background square. Make 4 matching units.

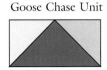

Diagonal Seams Diagrams

2. Lay out 4 Goose Chase units with 4 (2½" x 4½") rectangles that match background square. Join into squares as shown in *Pinwheel Block Assembly Diagram*; join squares to complete Pinwheel block as shown in *Pinwheel Block Diagram*.

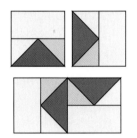

Pinwheel Block Assembly Diagram

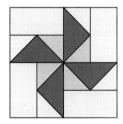

Pinwheel Block Diagram

3. Make 22 pinwheels for center and 68 pinwheels for outer area. Vary colors and group them as desired.

4. Join 4 (2½" x 4½") background rectangles into a 4½" x 8½" center spacer unit. Make 6 spacer units.

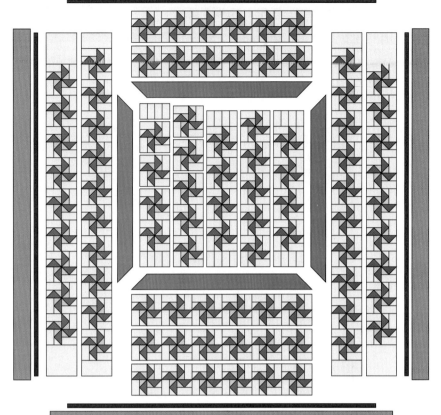

Quilt Top Assembly Diagram

5. Lay out center pinwheels in 5 vertical rows as shown in *Quilt Top Assembly Diagram*, with 6 spacer units at ends of first, third, and fifth rows. Arrange into color bands (see photo). When satisfied with placement, join into vertical rows. Join rows to complete center.

6. Add 1 green inner border to each side of center. Miter corners.

7. Arrange outer area pinwheels around center as shown. Join into sections as shown. Add 1 (4½" x 8½") spacer to each end of 2 (10-pinwheel) vertical rows. Add 1 (8½"-square) spacer to each end of 2 (9-pinwheel) vertical rows. Join

sections as shown. Join top and bottom sections to quilt center; then join side sections.

8. Add red borders to each side of quilt. Add red top and bottom borders.

9. Add green borders to each side of quilt. Add green top and bottom borders.

Quilting

Machine- or hand-quilt all pinwheel areas in Baptist fans. Quilt inner border with a swag pattern, and meander-quilt outer green border.

Finished Edges

Bind with straight-grain or bias binding made from green print.

Bee
Quilters

Letort Quilters
Carlisle, Pennsylvania

$\mathcal{T}$he 142-member Letort Quilters is an active group. "This guild is truly amazing, and its members are always working on something," says member Karen Kay Buckley, a nationally known quilting author. And although the guild's members have a lot of fun, they also do a lot of community service and charity work.

Money made from annual block exchanges and raffle quilts benefits shelters, local police, children's charities, and hospice programs. The proceeds from *Mariner's Rose Compass* will go to an area hospice program. "In fact," says Karen, "the honorarium from Oxmoor House will also go to our charities."

Mariner's Rose Compass
1997

Two guild members, Janet Shultzabarger and Karen Kay Buckley, designed this gorgeous quilt. Karen and Janet selected, washed, and ironed the fabrics. A small group volunteered to assemble the kits, which were distributed to members to piece. After the top was assembled, it was passed on to other members to quilt.

In all, more than 50 guild members worked on *Mariner's Rose Compass,* which is featured on our cover. It was given away in a drawing in June 1998.

Mariner's Rose Compass

Finished Quilt Size
101" x 101"

Number of Blocks and Finished Size
13 blocks   14" x 14"

Fabric Requirements
1½ yards red print for blocks (A) and border

1¼ yards medium blue print for blocks (D)

4½ yards dark blue print for blocks (F), border, binding

½ yard gold print for blocks (E)

⅛ yard rose print for blocks (G)

7 yards cream-on-white print for blocks (B, C), compass background, and appliqué setting triangles

3¾ yards cream-on-cream print for sashing and appliquéd border

1¾ yards dark green print #1 for vines

1 yard dark green print #2 for bud bases (I)

¾ yard each of 2 different medium green prints for leaves (H)

½ yard pink print for folded rosebuds

½ yard dark pink print for folded rosebuds

½ yard red solid for folded rosebuds

9 yards floral print backing (or 3 yards of 108"-wide backing)

Pieces to Cut
Red print
- 8 (2½"-wide) crosswise strips. Piece to make 4 border strips.
- 208 As.

Medium blue print
- 104 Ds.

Dark blue print
- 1 yard for binding.
- 3 yards. Cut 4 (6½"-wide) lengthwise strips for outer border.
- 104 Fs.

Gold print
- 104 Es.

Rose print
- 13 Gs, centered on a rose.

Cream-on-white print
- 7 (14½"-wide) crosswise strips. Cut strips into 13 (14½") squares for compass backgrounds.
- 1 (21¼"-wide) crosswise strip. Cut strip into 2 (21¼") squares. Cut squares in quarters diagonally to make 8 quarter-square triangles for side setting triangles.

- 1 (11"-wide) crosswise strip. Cut strip into 2 (11") squares. Cut squares in half diagonally to make 4 half-square triangles for corner setting triangles.
- 416 Bs.
- 208 Cs.

Cream-on-cream print
- 2⅞ yards. Cut 9 (4½"-wide) lengthwise strips. Cut into:
  * 4 (4½" x 92") borders.
  * 2 (4½" x 96") sashing strips.
  * 2 (4½" x 60") sashing strips.
  * 2 (4½" x 25") sashing strips.
  * 9 (4½" x 14½") sashing strips.
- 5 (4½"-wide) crosswise strips. Cut into 9 (4½" x 14½") sashing strips.

102

Dark green print #1

- Cut 360" of 1⅛"-wide bias strips, piecing as needed to make 4 (90"-long) strip. Fold and press to make ⅜"-wide bias for border vines.
- Cut 950" of ¾"-wide bias strips, piecing as needed to make 4 (94"-long) strips, 4 (58"-long) strips, 4 (22"-long) strips, plus setting block strips. Fold and press to make ¼"-wide bias for sashing and setting block vines.

Dark green print #2

- 232 Is.

Medium green prints

- 616 Hs, half from each print.

Pink print

- 5 (2½"-wide) crosswise strips. Cut strips into 72 (2½") squares for folded rosebuds.

Dark pink print

- 5 (2½"-wide) crosswise strips. Cut strips into 80 (2½") squares for folded rosebuds.

Red solid

- 5 (2½"-wide) crosswise strips. Cut strips into 80 (2½") squares for folded rosebuds.

Block Assembly

Refer to *Block Assembly Diagram* throughout.

1. Join 2 Bs to sides of 1 A. Add 1 C to base as shown. Make 16 A/B/C units.

2. Join 2 A/B/C units to sides of 1 D. Make 8 A/B/C/D units.

3. Join 2 A/B/C/D units to sides of 1 F. Make 4 units.

4. Join 2 Es to 1 F as shown. Make 4 E/F units.

5. Working in a circle, join units as shown to complete

points. Appliqué 1 G in center to complete compass.

6. Appliqué compass in center of 1 (14½") background square to complete block. Trim background fabric underneath to reduce bulk.

7. Make 13 blocks (*Block Diagram*).

Quilt Top Assembly

1. Referring to *Quilt Smart* on page 104, use 2½" squares to make 232 folded rosebuds.

2. Referring to *Side Triangle Appliqué Diagram*, appliqué 1 (7"), 2 (5"), 2 (2¾") vines; 20 leaves; and 5 rosebuds and bases (I) to each side setting triangle. In quilt shown, each triangle has 1 pink, 2 dark pink, and 2 red

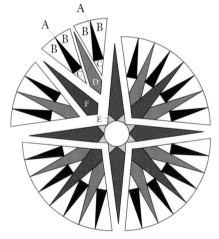

Block Assembly Diagram

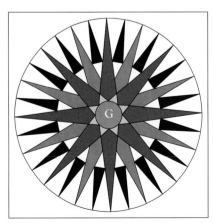

Block Diagram

rosebuds, and each set of 2 leaves has 1 of each print.

3. Referring to *Corner Triangle Appliqué Diagram*, appliqué 1 (4½") and 2 (3") vines, 10 leaves, and 3 rosebuds (1 of each color) with bases (I) to each corner setting triangle.

4. Arrange blocks, setting triangles and sashing as shown in *Quilt Top Assembly Diagram*. Join in diagonal rows; join rows to complete center.

5. Using photo as a guide, appliqué vines, rosebuds, and leaves onto sashing. Appliqué vines from top left to bottom right sections first. There are 3 rosebuds (1 of each color) on each side of each block. Each leaf pair has 1 leaf from each print. Each interior intersection has 4 leaves.

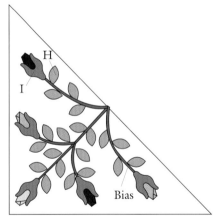

Side Triangle Appliqué Diagram

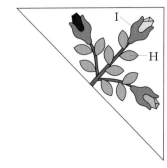

Corner Triangle Appliqué Diagram

6. Add 1 red border, centered, to each side of quilt. Miter corners.

7. Repeat with cream border and blue border.

8. Appliqué each cream border with 1 vine, 38 leaves, and 18 rosebuds (6 of each color).

Quilting

Quilt each compass through every point and in-the-ditch around each block. Quilt in-the-ditch around each appliqué and outline-quilt ¼" from each appliqué. Quilt red border in an orange peel design. Quilt blue border in 1⅝" stripes.

Finished Edges

Bind with straight-grain or bias binding made from dark blue print.

Quilt Top Assembly Diagram

❖QUILT SMART❖
Folded Rosebuds

1. Cut square in indicated size (in this quilt, 2½"). Fold square in half with wrong sides facing (*Diagram 1*).

2. Fold each side toward center, overlapping as shown in *Diagram 2*. Baste along bottom edges of bud to secure.

3. *For a gathered folded rosebud,* use running stitches to secure fold together. Gently gather raw edges of rosebud

to fit inside rosebud base (*Diagram 3*).

4. Appliqué in place, covering raw edges with bud base (*Diagram 1*). You may also

secure the rose just at the base, and then appliqué base in position, leaving folded edges of bud top free.

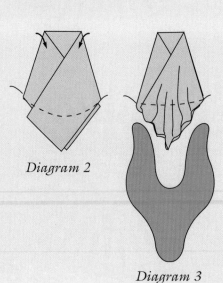

Diagram 2

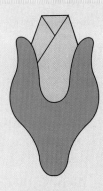

Diagram 4

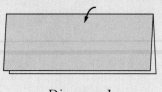

Diagram 1

Diagram 3

Shown at right are the Rhapsody in Blue *committee members: Marion Watchinski, Emily Senuta, Doreen Perkins, Joan Streck, and chairperson Susan Sommerlath.*

Blue Valley Quilt Guild
Stanley, Kansas

The Blue Valley Quilt Guild is not unlike other guilds in its format. On the first Tuesday of each month, members gather at the Stanley Presbyterian Church for fun, food, and fellowship. After a short business meeting comes show and tell and a program. Members also enjoy other activities such as field trips and potluck dinners. And, of course, they do their share of charity work.

But it's in the production of their opportunity quilt that they truly stand apart. Every aspect of the quilt is planned and executed with great attention to detail. The first step for the five-member committee is an initial design meeting. In 1995, each committee member was charged with the task of coming up with design possiblities for a medallion quilt. At their second meeting, Emily Senuta's design, *Rhapsody in Blue,* was chosen.

"Then we went shopping for fabric," says Emily. The committee put together kits to be distributed to guild members, who turned Emily's design into the beautiful finished quilt you see here.

Rhapsody in Blue
1996

Each year, members of the Blue Valley Quilt Guild make an opportunity quilt, which they raffle to raise funds to help support the guild's activities and charity work. The 1996 quilt, *Rhapsody in Blue,* garnered an impressive $2,600 in ticket sales.

In all, 52 Blue Valley quilters lent their talents to this masterpiece. It has been shown in several quilt and craft shows, including Silver Dollar City in 1996. It also appears in the American Quilter's Society's *1999 Quilt Art Engagement Calendar.*

The proud owner of the the quilt is Janice Woodring of Springfield, Missouri.

Rhapsody in Blue

Finished Quilt Size
84" x 84"

Number of Blocks and Finished Size
72 blocks   6" x 6"

Fabric Requirements
1 yard blue stripe for appliqué, border, and binding

½ yard blue/green/rose print for border centers

½ yard black background with brights and gold metallic for diamond border

1½ yards green-with-black print for bias, vines, and leaves

3¾ yards total assorted blue and green prints for appliqué and borders

1 yard total assorted red/rose prints for appliqué flowers

½ yard total assorted blue and blue/purple/red prints for appliqué flowers

⅛ yard mottled blue for appliqué flower centers

8 yards mottled tan print for background

7½ yards fabric for backing (or 2½ yards of 90"-wide fabric)

Pieces to Cut
Blue stripe
- 8 (⅞"-wide) crosswise strips. Piece strips to make 4 (⅞" x 74") border strips.
- 9 (2¼"-wide) crosswise strips for binding.
- Use remainder for leaf appliqué.

Blue/green/rose print
- 4 (2⅝"-wide) crosswise strips. Cut strips into 52 (2⅝") squares for block centers (U).

Black background with brights and gold metallic
- 5 (2"-wide) crosswise strips. Cut strips into 100 (2") squares for diamond border.

Green-with-black print
- Cut 1 (23½") square. Follow instructions on page 144 to make approximately 440" of ¾"-wide bias. Fold and press to make ¼"-wide bias. Cut bias into the following pieces:
  *4 (4½"-long) pieces for center.
  *4 (10"-long) pieces for center.
  *8 (15"-long) pieces for center corner blocks.
  *8 (7"-long) pieces for center corner blocks.
  *4 (5"-long) pieces for center corner blocks.
  *8 (11"-long) pieces for border center appliqué.

*8 (14½"-long) pieces for border vines.
- 8 A rev.
- 8 As.
- 4 B rev.
- 4 Gs.
- 4 G rev.
- 4 Hs.
- 8 Is.
- 8 I rev.

Assorted blue and green prints
- 288 Ys for blocks
- 48 As.
- 48 A rev.
- 44 Bs.
- 44 B rev.
- 28 Cs.
- 20 C rev.
- 32 Ds.
- 24 D rev.
- 16 Es.
- 20 E rev.
- 24 Fs.
- 16 F rev.

Assorted red/rose prints
- •20 large petals.
- •20 medium petals.
- •20 small petals.
- •100 tiny petals.

Assorted blue and blue/purple/red prints
- •Large petals—4 blue and 8 blue/purple/red.
- •Medium petals—4 blue and 8 blue/purple/red.
- •Small petals—4 blue and 8 blue/purple/red.
- •Tiny petals—20 blue and 40 blue/purple/red.

Mottled blue
- •4 large centers.
- •4 medium centers.
- •4 small centers.
- •20 tiny centers.

Mottled tan print
- •1 (24½") square for center appliqué background.
- •2 (26½") squares. Cut squares in half diagonally to make 4 half-square triangles for center corner appliqué backgrounds.
- •12 (8½"-wide) crosswise strips. Cut strips into 4 (8½" x 32½") center border sections and 8 (8½" x 28") left and right border sections. These will be joined and mitered when added to quilt.
- •22 (2"-wide) crosswise strips. Cut strips into 128 (2" x 6½") rectangles (T).
- •3 (2"-wide) crosswise strips. Cut strips into 8 Zs and 8 Z rev. for corner blocks.
- •5 (2¾"-wide) crosswise strips. Cut strips into 68 (2¾") squares. Cut squares in quarters diagonally to make 272 quarter-square triangles (V).
- •1 (2⅜"-wide) crosswise strip. Cut strip into 4 (2⅜")

squares. Cut squares in half diagonally to make 8 half-square triangles (W).
- •1 (2"-wide) crosswise strip. Cut strip into 8 (2") squares (X) for corner blocks.
- •2 (2⅝"-wide) crosswise strips. Cut strips into 20 (2⅝") squares (U).
- •4 (3⅜"-wide) crosswise strips. Cut strips into 50 (3⅜") squares. Cut squares in quarters diagonally to make 200 quarter-square triangles for diamond border.

Appliqué Flower Assembly

Each flower has 1 blue petal with 1 blue/purple/red petal on each side. Remaining 5 petals are red/rose. Orient flowers as shown in photo. Position first petal and appliqué down top right edge only. Position next petal and appliqué entire left edge and top right edge. Continue working clockwise until last petal is added. For last petal, tuck right edge under first petal and then appliqué both.

Block Assembly

1. Referring to *Tiny Flower Diagram*, appliqué 8 tiny petals and 1 tiny center for flower on each of 20 tan U squares, as instructed above.

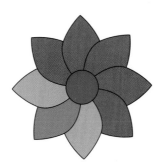

Tiny Flower Diagram (shown actual size)

2. Referring to *Block Assembly Diagram*, join 1 tan V to 1 Y. Repeat to make 2 right units and 2 left units. Join 1 unit to each side of 1 appliquéd U as shown. Set in seam between Y pieces. Join 1 T to each side to complete block as shown in *Block Diagram*. Make 16 straight blocks with appliquéd tan U and 48 straight blocks with blue/green/rose U.

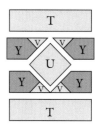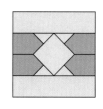

Block Assembly Diagram   *Block Diagram*

3. Referring to *Corner Block Assembly Diagram*, join 1 V triangle to 1 Y to make 1 left unit. Repeat to make 1 right unit. Join to opposite sides of 1 appliquéd U. Join 2 Y units along short sides. Add to 1 side of U as shown. Set in X square. Add 1 W to remaining U side. Join 1 Z and 1 Z rev. to each side to complete corner block, setting in corner seam.

4. Make 4 corner blocks as shown in *Corner Block Diagram* with appliquéd tan U and 4 corner blocks with blue/green/rose U.

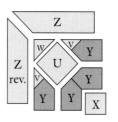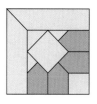

Corner Block Assembly Diagram   *Corner Block Diagram*

Quilt Top Assembly

1. Referring to *¼ Center Appliqué Diagram*, appliqué pieces in order: 4 As, 8 A rev., 12 Bs, 4 B rev., 8 Cs, 4 Ds, 4 D rev., 32 large petals, 4 large centers, 4 (10") bias strips, and 4 (4½"-long) bias strips.

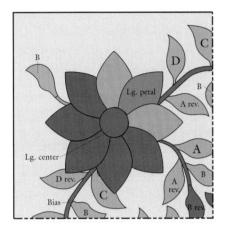

¼ Center Appliqué Diagram

2. Join 4 straight blocks with appliquéd tiny flowers into a strip. Make 2 strips. Add to opposite sides of appliquéd center square. Join 4 straight blocks and 2 corner blocks into a strip as shown in *Quilt Top Assembly Diagram*. Make 2 strips. Add to remaining sides of center.

3. Referring to *Center Corner Appliqué Diagram*, appliqué each corner triangle with 4 As, 4 A rev., 4 Bs, 4 B rev., 2 Cs, 2 C rev., 4 Ds, 2 D

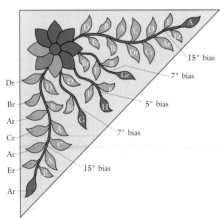

Center Corner Appliqué Diagram

Quilt Top Assembly Diagram

rev., 2 Es, 3 E rev., 2 Fs, 1 G, 1 G rev., 1 H, 2 (15"-long) bias pieces, 2 (7"-long) bias pieces, and 1 (5"-long) bias piece. Add 8 medium petals and 1 medium center to each corner triangle.

4. Add appliquéd triangles to center.

5. Join 1 tan quarter-square triangle to each side of 1 black square as shown in *Diamond Border Assembly Diagram*. Make 96 units. Join into 4 strips of 24 units. Add 2 triangles to 1 square as shown for end unit. Make 4 end units and add 1 to each strip. Add 1 strip to each side of center for diamond border.

6. Referring to *Border Center Appliqué Diagram*, appliqué each (8½" x 33") center border piece with 5 As, 5 A

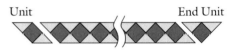

Diamond Border Assembly Diagram

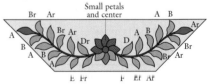

Border Center Appliqué Diagram

Left Border Appliqué Diagram

rev., 4 Bs, 4 B rev., 1 D, 1 D rev., 1 E, 1 E rev., 1 F, 1 F rev., 8 small petals, 1 small center, and 2 (11"-long) bias pieces.

7. Referring to *Left Border Appliqué Diagram*, appliqué each left border with 3 As, 2 Bs, 1 B rev., 1 C, 2 C rev., 2 D rev.,

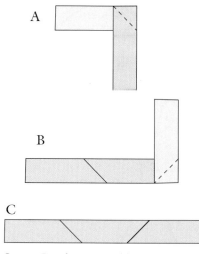

Outer Border Assembly Diagrams

1 E rev., 3 Fs, 1 I, 1 I rev., and 2 (14½"-long) bias pieces.

8. Appliqué each right border piece as a mirror image of left border piece with 3 A rev., 1 B, 2 B rev., 2 Cs, 1 C rev., 2 Ds, 1 E, 3 F rev., 1 I, 1 I rev.

9. Referring to *Outer Border Assembly Diagrams*, join 1 left and 1 right border piece to 1 center border piece using diagonal seams. Repeat for all 4 borders. Add 1 border to each side, mitering corners.

10. Add 1 stripe border to each side, mitering corners.

11. Join 12 straight border blocks into a strip. Make 4

strips. Add 1 strip to sides of quilt. Add 2 corner blocks to each end of remaining strips and add to top and bottom of quilt.

Quilting

Outline-quilt around all appliqué except tiny flowers. Fill appliqué background with echoed diamonds from center. Quilt each block with flower pattern, and quilt diamond border in-the-ditch.

Finished Edges

Bind with straight-grain or bias binding made from blue stripe.

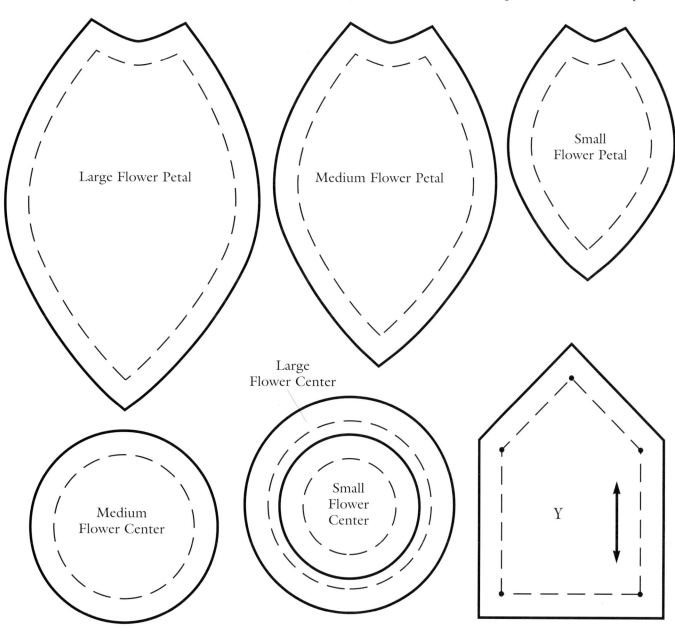

111

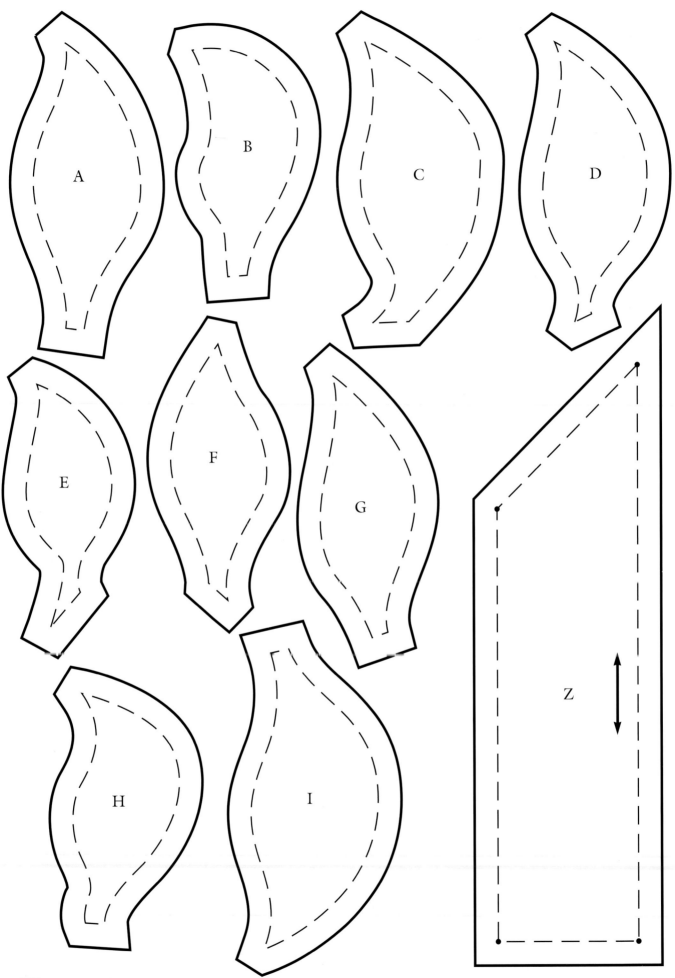

Hands All Around Bee
Downers Grove, Illinois

This small bee is a sub-group of the 150-member Faithful Circle Quilt Guild, which was founded in 1974. The guild meets once a month at the First Presbyterian Church of Downers Grove. In the meantime, members of the Hands All Around Bee get together to quilt and plan fun projects like the round-robin challenge that produced the quilt shown here.

Judy Teska is a member of the bee and the originator and owner of the quilt.

Round Robin Medallion
1997

Some people call them wonder fabrics, some call them dogs, and some just call them eye sores—those fat quarters, half yards, even yardages that are just too weird, boring, or ugly to use in our quilts. We often wonder why we ever bought them in the first place.

Well, the Hands All Around Bee figured out how to use their wonder fabrics, and just look at the results—anything but ugly!

The group gathered all their unattractive prints and divided them into four groups. Using four different colors of Rit Dye®—dark rose, gold, blue, and green—they overdyed their prints and divided them equally among the 12 bee members.

Then the bee organized into three groups of four each. The challenge was to make a round-robin project using these overdyed dogs.

"We could add additional fabrics if we wished," says Judy Teska, the originator and owner of the quilt shown on the next page.

After Judy finished her center square of dimensional flowers, members Jill Bates, Marlene Schellenberg, and Adrienne Danko added concentric borders. They then gave the finished top back to Judy for quilting.

Judy's quilt won First Place in the wall-hanging category in the Faithful Circle Quilt Guild's 1997 quilt show.

Round Robin Medallion

Finished Quilt Size
37" x 37"

Number of Blocks and Finished Size
1 appliqué block   14¾" x 14¾"
44 Hourglass blocks 1¾" x 1¾"

Fabric Requirements
½ yard beige solid for appliqué
     background
¼ yard blue print for bowl and
     patchwork*
¼ yard green print for border and
     patchwork*
¼ yard gold print for border
     squares and patchwork*
¼ yard rose print for diamonds
     and patchwork*
½ yard dark blue solid for inner
     borders
¾ yard dark blue print for
     appliquéd border
¾ yard green solid for vines
1¾ yards total assorted prints for
     patchwork and appliqué (rose,
     mauve, gold-and-black, gold,
     green, blue)
¾ yard black for binding
1¼ yards blue print for backing

*If you wish to use overdyed
fabrics as Judy Teska and her bee
sisters did, you'll also need 4
packages of Rit Dye: blue, green,
gold, and dark rose. Choose any
4 (¼-yard) fabrics from your
stash. Following directions on dye
package, dye each ¼ yard a different color.

Other Materials
Green embroidery floss
Polyester stuffing

Pieces to Cut
Beige solid
  • 1 (15¼") square for center
    appliqué background.
Blue print
  • 1 bowl (A).
Green print
  • 2 (1⅝"-wide) crosswise strips.
    Cut strips into 4 (1⅝" x
    15¼") inner border strips.
Gold print
  • 4 (1⅝") squares for corner
    squares.
Rose print
  • 4 diamonds for border (D).
Dark blue solid
  • 2 (¾"-wide) crosswise strips.
    Cut strips into 2 (¾" x 17½")
    border strips and 2 (¾" x
    18") border strips.
  • 3 (1"-wide) crosswise strips.
    Cut strips into 2 (1" x 21½")
    border strips and 2 (1" x
    22½") border strips.

  • 4 (1½"-wide) crosswise strips.
    Cut strips into 2 (1½" x
    23½") border strips and 2
    (1½" x 25½") border strips.
Dark blue print
  • 4 (5½"-wide) crosswise strips.
    Cut strips into 2 (5½" x
    27½") rectangles and 2 (5½"
    x 37½") rectangles for
    appliquéd border.
Green solid
  • Cut ⅝"-wide bias strips, piec-
    ing as needed to make 28".
    Fold and press to make ³⁄₁₆"-
    wide finished bias for stems.
  • Cut 1⅛"-wide bias strips,
    piecing as needed to make 2
    (45"-long) strips. Fold and
    press to make ⅜"-wide fin-
    ished bias for vines.
Assorted prints plus scraps from
     above
  • 3" squares for Hourglass
    blocks. Cut squares in quar-

114

ters diagonally to make 4 quarter square triangles. You will need 88 sets of 2 triangles to make 44 blocks, so you will need as few as 44 squares or as many as 88 squares, depending on how many repeats you desire.

- 45–50 random length (2"–5") 1"-wide rectangles for narrow spiral border.
- 42 (1½" x 4¼") rectangles for wide spiral border.
- 22 (1¼" x 25") strips for ruched roses. Quilt shown has 5 gold-and-black print, 6 blue, 8 gold, and 3 red roses.
- 22 (1¾") squares for folded rosebuds.
- 22 rosebud bases (B).
- 72 small leaves (C).
- 18 border leaves (E).

Quilt Top Assembly

1. Referring to *Quilt Smart* on pages 104 and 117, make 22 folded rosebuds and 22 ruched roses.

2. Appliqué bowl (A), 9 folded rosebuds with bases (B), 72 leaves (C), and 14 ruched roses as shown in *Appliqué Placement Diagram* onto beige background square. In this quilt,

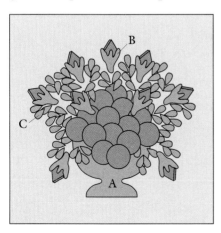

Appliqué Placement Diagram

Stemstitch Diagram

folded edges of rosebuds are not stitched down for dimensional effect. Stemstitch rose stems after appliqué is complete.

3. Add 2 green print border strips to sides of block. Add 1 gold corner square to each end of remaining green print border strips. Add to top and bottom.

4. Appliqué 1 diamond (D) onto center of each border, adding a small amount of stuffing before closing.

5. Add 1 (¾" x 17½") blue border strip to top and bottom of quilt. Add 1 (¾" x 18") blue border strip to sides of quilt.

6. Choose 2 sets of 2 matching quarter-square triangles. Join 1 of each as shown in *Hourglass Assembly Diagram* to make a half-square unit; repeat. Join to make 1 Hourglass block as shown in *Hourglass Block Diagram*. Make 44 blocks.

Hourglass Assembly Diagram

Hourglass Block Diagram

7. Join Hourglass blocks into strips as shown in photo. Make 2 (10-block) strips and 2 (12-block) strips. Join 1 (10-block) strip to each side of quilt. Join remaining strips to top and bottom of quilt.

8. Add 1 (1" x 21½") blue border strip to top and bottom of quilt. Add 1 (1" x 22½") blue border strip to sides of quilt.

9. To make narrow spiral border, refer to *Spiral Border Diagrams*. Using diagonal seams, join random length 1"-wide rectangles into a strip as shown. Make 2 (22½"-long) strips and join to sides of quilt, noting direction of angle. Make 2 (23½"-long) strips, matching end colors to end colors on side strips. Add to top and bottom of quilt.

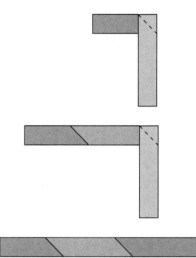

Spiral Border Diagrams

10. Add 1 (1½" x 23½") blue border strip to top and bottom of quilt. Add 1 (1½" x 25½") blue border strip to sides of quilt.

11. To make wide spiral border, repeat Step 9 with (1½" x 4¼") rectangles, matching corner colors. Make 2 (1½" x 25½") strips and 2 (1½" x 27½") strips; add to quilt.

12. Add 1 (5½" x 27½") blue border strip to sides of quilt. Add 1 (5½" x 37½") blue border strip to top and bottom of quilt.

13. Using photo as a guide, appliqué bias stems, bias vines, 13 folded rosebuds with bases (B), 18 leaves (E), and 8 ruched roses to blue border.

Quilting

Fill center block background with machine stipple quilting. Quilt in-the-ditch around each border and through each Hourglass block. Stipple-quilt background of blue appliquéd border.

Finished Edges

Bind with straight-grain or bias binding made from black.

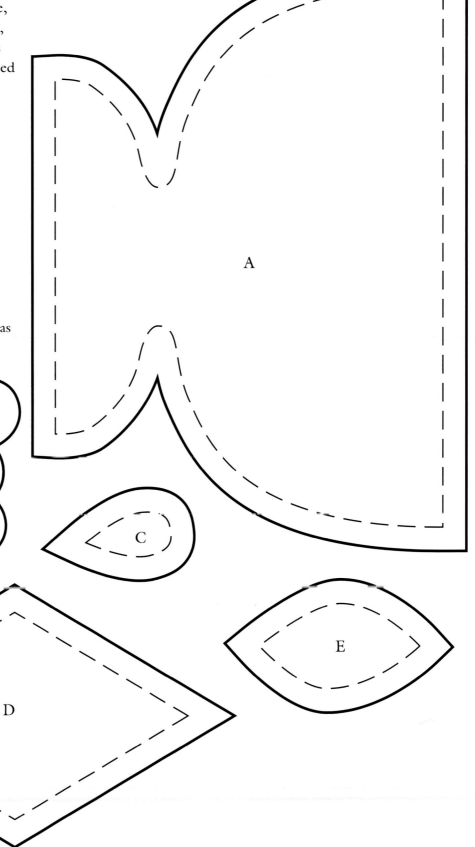

❖QUILT SMART❖

Ruched Roses

1. Cut 1 (1¼"-wide) strip. With wrong sides facing, fold down ¼" and baste along 1 long edge. Repeat on other long edge so that raw edges meet in the center (*Diagram 1*).

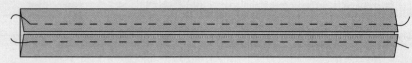

Diagram 1

2. Using a pencil and Marking Guide, make marks 1" apart along folded edges, alternating sides. Referring to *Diagram 2*, run a gathering thread in a zigzag design from mark to mark.

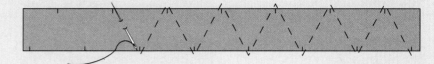

Diagram 2

3. Turn under beginning edge and secure. Begin gathering thread, as shown in *Diagram 3*. Arrange first few petals into a circle and tack together, gathering as you progress. Tack each row to previous row as you progress. On last petal, pull gathering thread tight and knot. Tuck remaining end under rose.

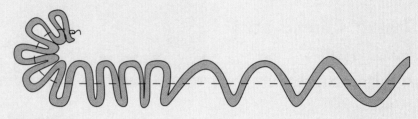

Diagram 3

4. Appliqué ruched rose to background.

Marking Guide

117

Seated (left to right) are Flying Geese and Goslings members Barbara Rennard, Jayne Schlosser, and Deb Hickman. Standing are Sandy Harris and Claudia Swee.

Flying Geese and Goslings
Omaha, Nebraska

This bee began 12 years ago as a quilting/play group—five young mothers who shared an interest in quilting.

"The kids would play, and we would work on our projects," says Barbara Rennard.

The "goslings" are all pretty much grown up now, but the group still meets once a week at each other's homes to quilt and exchange ideas.

"Recently we assembled and quilted two wedding quilts for my children," says Barbara, "the first of our former goslings to marry." The quilt shown here is one of those wedding quilts.

That Blanket Thing
1995

"Many hands make light work" could be the motto of Flying Geese and Goslings. These five women have set as a goal to make a wedding quilt for each of their collective 17 children.

Barbara Rennard's two children, former goslings, are married now and have their wedding quilts. The group made the quilt shown here for Barbara's daughter and son-in-law, Rachel and Jonathan Witherspoon.

"Because everyone helped," says Barbara, "the project became much less daunting."

Jonathan, not having had an appreciation of quilting nurtured within him as his wife had, refers to the quilt as "that blanket thing." Barbara decided to adopt Jonathan's description as the official name of this quilt, which is actually a Single Wedding Ring adaptation.

That Blanket Thing

Finished Quilt Size
90¼" x 104½"

Number of Blocks and Finished Size
30 blocks   10" x 10"

Fabric Requirements
3¾ yards total assorted light,
    medium, and dark blue prints
6½ yards white-on-white print
2¾ yards white-on-cream print
8¼ yards fabric for backing [3
    (2¾-yard) lengths]

Pieces to Cut
Assorted light, medium and dark
blue prints
- 23 (2⅞"-wide) crosswise strips
  to make half-square triangle A
  units.
- 8 (2½"-wide) crosswise strips.
  Cut strips into 120 (2½")
  squares for blocks (B).
- 10 (2¼") assorted crosswise
  strips for binding.
- 2 (2⅛") crosswise strips for
  6¼" corner blocks.
- 1 (1¾"-wide) crosswise strip.
  Cut strip into 16 (1¾")
  squares for corner blocks.

White-on-white print
- 2⅝ yards. Cut 4 (2"-wide)
  lengthwise strips. Cut 2 (2" x
  71¼") top and bottom inner
  borders and 2 (2" x 88⅜")
  side inner borders.
- Remainder is approximately
  34" wide. From remainder,
  cut crosswise:
  *5 (10½"-wide) strips. Cut
  strips into 15 (10½") squares
  for setting blocks (X).

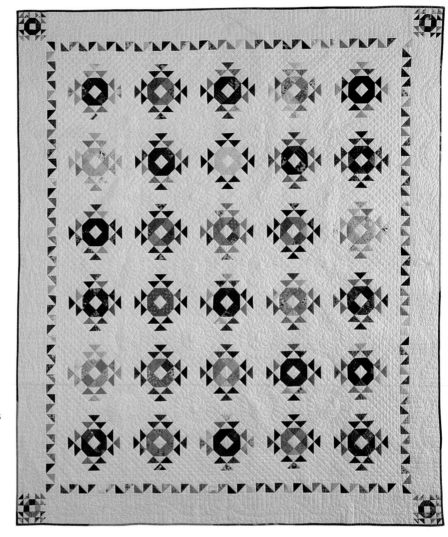

*1 (8⅜"-wide) strip. Cut strip
into 2 (8⅜") squares. Cut
squares in half diagonally to
make 4 corner triangles (Y).
*12 (2½"-wide) strips. Cut
strips into 150 (2½") squares
for blocks (B).
- 3 (16¼"-wide) crosswise
  strips. Cut strips into 5
  (16¼") squares. Cut squares
  in quarters diagonally to make
  18 side setting triangles (Z).
  You will have 2 extra.
- 23 (2⅞"-wide) crosswise strips
  to make half-square triangle A
  units.
- 2 (2⅛"-wide) crosswise strips
  for 6¼" corner blocks.

- 1 (1¾"-wide) crosswise strip.
  Cut strip into 20 (1¾")
  squares for corner blocks.
- Cut 4 (1⅜" x 2½") spacer
  strips for top and bottom
  inner borders.

White-on-cream print
- 4 (6¾"-wide) lengthwise
  strips. Cut 2 (6¾" x 78¼")
  strips and 2 (6¾" x 92½")
  strips for outer borders.

Quilt Top Assembly
1. Refer to *Quilt Smart*
method for making half-square
triangles on page 11. Match 1
(2⅞") blue strip to 1 (2⅞")
white-on-white strip. Stitch, cut,
and press. Repeat to make 644

blue-and-white half-square tri-angle units (A).

2. To make 1 (10") Single Wedding Ring block, choose 16 assorted A units and 4 (2½") assorted blue B squares. Lay out as shown in *Block Assembly Diagram* with 5 white-on-white 2½" B squares. Join into rows; join rows to complete block as shown in *Block Diagram*.

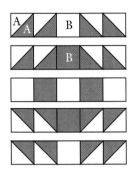

Block Assembly Diagram

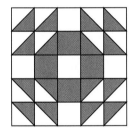

Block Diagram

3. Make 30 blocks.

4. Lay out blocks with set-ting blocks and triangles as shown in *Quilt Top Assembly Diagram*. Join into diagonal rows; join rows to complete quilt center.

5. Add 1 (2" x 71¼") white-on-white border to top and bot-tom of quilt.

6. Add 1 (2" x 88⅜") white-on-white border to sides of quilt.

7. Join 36 A units into a strip as shown in *Quilt Top Assembly Diagram*. Add 1 (1⅜" x 2½") spacer strip to each end.

Quilt Top Assembly Diagram

Repeat. Add to top and bottom of quilt.

8. Join 46 A units into a strip as shown in *Quilt Top Assembly Diagram*. Repeat. Add to sides of quilt.

9. Add 1 (6¾" x 92½") white-on-cream border to each side of quilt.

10. To make corner blocks, first make half-square triangles in same manner as above, using 2⅛" strips and marking squares, to make 64 half-square triangle units. Make 4 (6¼") Single Wedding Ring blocks as described above, using 1¾" squares in place of Bs. Join 1 block to each end of remaining

white-on-cream border strips. Add to top and bottom of quilt.

Quilting

Quilt in-the-ditch in each block and fill with a grid in outer white areas. Quilt a feathered wreath in each setting block. Fill setting tri-angles and inner white borders with a grid. Quilt in-the-ditch in each border unit. Quilt a feather pattern in each border and fill with a stripe pattern. Quilt corner blocks in-the-ditch.

Finished Edges

Bind with straight-grain or bias binding made from several blue prints.

Nancy Judd, shown at right, won Trinity Valley Waltz in 1992 at the Trinity Valley Quilt Show in Fort Worth, Texas.

Trinity Valley Quilters' Guild
Fort Worth, Texas

Trinity Valley Quilters' Guild was conceived in a quilting class in 1981. The 12 women attending that class decided they would like to form an organization where quilters could meet regularly to share their interest in the craft. They worked and planned for the next four months, and on January 15, 1982, the guild's first meeting took place.

"Only 21 women attended that first meeting," says 1998 guild president Jacque Hensell. "Membership now exceeds 350."

The guild's community service projects include donating books to local libraries, baby quilts to an area hospital, and funds and supplies to women's shelters. Guild funds also provide college scholarships to students of textile studies.

Trinity Valley Waltz
1992

The two block designs in this quilt are traditionally known as 54-40 or Fight! and Snowball. While the quilt actually contains no curved seams, the juxtaposition of these two blocks causes an illusion of curves.

Terri Ellis and Cynthia Boatman, who chaired the Trinity Valley Quilter's Guild donation quilt committee in 1991, found inspiration for this quilt in Judy Martin's book *Scrap Quilts*.

"The pattern in the book called for 14" blocks," says Jacque Hensell. "But the committee scaled the pattern down to 9" blocks."

The committee supplied background muslin for the quilt, and participating guild members supplied the scraps for the blocks. The name of the quilt was adapted from Judy Martin's quilt, says Jacque, which was *Tennessee Waltz*.

Trinity Valley Waltz

Finished Quilt Size
81" x 99"

Number of Blocks and Finished Size
63 blocks   9" x 9"

  32 54-40 or Fight blocks and
  31 Snowball blocks

Fabric Requirements
3 yards total assorted scraps
4¾ yards white-on-cream print
3½ yards blue print
7½ yards fabric for backing

Pieces to Cut
Assorted scraps
- 600 (2") squares for 54-40 or Fight blocks and borders (C).
- 124 (3½") squares for Snowball blocks (D).

White-on-cream print
- 8 (9½"-wide) crosswise strips. Cut into 31 (9½") squares for Snowball blocks (E).
- 128 As.
- 13 (2"-wide) crosswise strips. Cut into 256 (2") squares for 54-40 or Fight blocks (C).
- 5 (3½"-wide) crosswise strips. Cut strips into 54 (3½") squares for border.

Blue print
- 18 (3½"-wide) crosswise strips. Piece to make:
  * 2 (3½" x 81½") inner side border strips.
  * 2 (3½" x 69½") inner top and bottom border strips.
  * 2 (3½" x 104") outer side border strips.
  * 2 (3½" x 85") outer top and bottom border strips.
- 128 Bs.
- 128 B rev.

Block Assembly
1. Join 1 B and 1 B rev. to each side of 1 A. Make 4 A/B units.

2. Join 1 print C and 1 white-on-cream C. Repeat. Join to make a four-patch C unit. Make 4 C white-and-print units.

3. Join 4 print Cs into a four-patch for 1 center C unit.

4. Referring to *54-40 or Fight Block Assembly Diagram*, lay out 4 A/B units, 4 C white-and-print units, and 1 center C unit. Join into rows; join rows to complete block as shown in *54-40 or Fight Block Diagram*. Make 32 blocks.

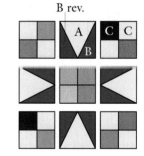

54-40 or Fight Block Assembly Diagram

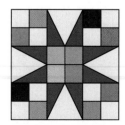

54-40 or Fight Block Diagram

5. Using diagonal seams, join 1 (3½") print square (D) to each corner of 1 (9½") white square (E) as shown in *Snowball Block Assembly Diagram*. Trim excess and press. Make 31 Snowball blocks.

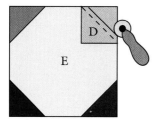

Snowball Block Assembly Diagram

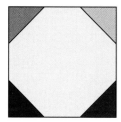

Snowball Block Diagram

Quilt Top Assembly

1. Alternate blocks in 9 horizontal rows of 7 blocks each, as shown in *Quilt Top Assembly Diagram*. Join into rows; join rows to complete center.

2. Add 1 (3½" x 81½") blue border to sides of quilt. Add blue top and bottom borders.

3. Join 4 print Cs into a four-patch. Make 54 border units.

4. Alternate 15 C units and 14 (3½") white squares. Join into a strip. Make 2 strips. Add to sides of quilt.

5. Alternate 12 C units and 13 (3½") white squares. Join into a strip. Make 2 strips. Add to top and bottom of quilt.

6. Add remaining blue borders to sides and then to top and bottom of quilt. Miter corners.

Quilt Top Assembly Diagram

Quilting

Outline-quilt ¼" inside each patch. Quilt a rose and leaf pattern in each white area. Quilt a leaf garland in each blue border.

Finished Edges

Bind with straight-grain or bias binding made from blue print.

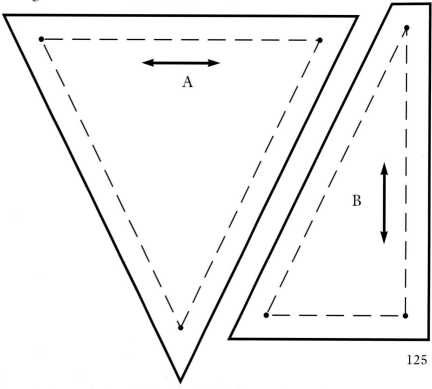

125

Designer Gallery

Sunbonnet Sues and Overall Sams stroll among 20 miniature masterpieces in this patchwork quilt show.

Rosemary Youngs
Walker, Michigan

Rosemary Youngs says she began toying with the idea of quilting in 1988 after visiting the quilt exhibit at the state fair. "I tried to teach myself to quilt, and learned a lot from my mistakes," she says.

"The best part of quiltmaking is the friendships we share."

But it wasn't until 1992 that she got serious. That's when she joined the West Michigan Quilt Guild and found the inspiration she needed to stop toying and start quilting in earnest.

"I jumped into the world of quilting, fabric, stencils, patterns, and book collecting," says Rosemary.

The best thing she has gained from quiltmaking is not the awards and recognition that her excellent work and charming designs have brought her. "The best part of quiltmaking is the friendships we share through the process of making our quilts," she says.

Great American Quilters and Their Quilts
1996

"This quilt will always be my favorite," says Rosemary. "I particularly enjoy appliqué, and my favorite pattern is Sunbonnet Sue."

Rosemary adds that she was inspired by the many different cultures represented in quiltmaking: traditional American, Amish, Hawaiian, African American, and others. She used the much-loved Sunbonnet Sue character to help her show these different cultures in this amazing quilt.

The quilt depicts an outdoor quilt show. Sunbonnet Sues and Overall Sams stroll among the miniature quilts, each a perfect replica of its full-size counterpart.

"I used reproduction fabrics to make them look authentic," says Rosemary. "As I made each row, I was thrilled and couldn't wait to get to the next row."

Eileen Bahring Sullivan
Alpharetta, Georgia

Eileen Sullivan is no stranger to recognition. Her quilts have won numerous awards at the American Quilter's Society show in Paducah, including two ribbons for First Place, Professional Division. She took Best of Show in Houston in both 1991 and 1993. Her work has been featured in most of the major quilting magazines, two calendars, and many books. And she has quilts in the permanent collections of two museums, including the Museum of the American Quilter's Society in Paducah.

Born and raised in Connecticut, Eileen has been quilting since 1979 and is familiar with many styles and techniques.

"My current work focuses on foundation piecing with freezer paper," says Eileen. She adds that she works in both traditional and contemporary styles.

Remembering Monet
1997

The title of this stunning quilt is an obvious allusion to a series of paintings by the French Impressionist, Claude Monet. Although its maker, Eileen Sullivan, has been quilting for many years, she has only recently started foundation piecing, the technique she used to make this beauty.

Eileen markets patterns for some of her original designs through The Designer's Workshop. Her patterns are carried in quilt shops all through the U.S. and abroad, and in several mail-order catalogs.

"Most of my patterns are floral in nature," says Eileen.

"All are foundation pieced on freezer paper."

To order patterns, write to The Designer's Workshop, P.O. Box 1026, Duluth, GA 30096. No pattern is available for *Remembering Monet* .

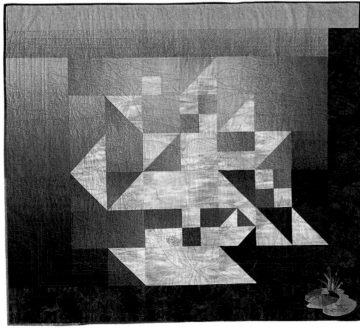

Eileen Sullivan's quilt (above) is reminiscent of the work of Impressionist painter Claude Monet. But its pieced back (left) is abstract in design.

B. Nicole Goffman
Pasadena, California

*F*ive years ago, Nicole Goffman gave up a 15-year business career to be a full-time mom to her teenage daughter.

"Then my daughter decided to live with her father," says Nicole. "I was lost. I didn't know what to do with myself."

She had always enjoyed drawing

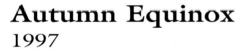

"Hand quilting is good therapy for me."

and painting, and had studied art in school. She also enjoyed sewing. After visiting a local quilt shop, she quickly realized that she could combine her artistic skills into a new and exciting experience—quiltmaking.

Nicole wasn't so much interested in traditional pieced quilts as in transferring her drawings into fabric using appliqué. And that's exactly what she does.

Nicole doesn't consider herself a professional—yet. "I quilt because I love it," she says. "I hope someday to be able to make a living at it."

Autumn Equinox
1997

Nicole Goffman must have enchanting dreams. "My fairy designs come from my dreams," she says. "In the morning I remember what I dreamed and draw the scenes."

Autumn Equinox is one in a series of four quilts that Nicole is making. "I've always loved the idea of fairies," she

says. In fact, her daughter grew up listening to Nicole tell bedtime stories of fairies, unicorns, and other creatures of fantasy.

"I feel there could be fairies that come out at different times of the year, attracted to certain plants and flowers," she adds. When finished, her four fairy quilts will depict a

different fairy for each season of the year.

Nicole says that fairies and quilting have been therapy for her, helping her adjust when her daughter left home. The fairies help her keep her connection with the innocent faith of children; quilting just makes her feel good.

"My fairy designs come from my dreams," says California quilt artist Nicole Goffman.

Cheryl Kerestes
Wyoming, Pennsylvania

*P*ennsylvania quilter Cheryl Kerestes remembers, as a teenager, visiting the quilt exhibits at the annual agricultural fair near her home.

"I loved those quilts and wanted to make one so badly," she recalls.

"There is so much in my life I wouldn't have, but for quilting."

Cheryl was only 18 when she started her first quilt, and it was slow going. "I didn't know anyone who knew how to quilt, and books and magazines on quilting were scarce."

But Cheryl persevered and finished her quilt. "That one was for my hope chest," she says. In the 20-something years since, she has made so many quilts, she's lost count.

Baltimore Album
1995

Some of the blocks in this quilt are copied from antique Baltimore Album quilts; some are completely original. Even to an educated eye, it's almost impossible to tell which is which.

The third block in the second horizontal row, for instance, is Cheryl's original creation. "It is a depiction of the 1775 Wyoming Monument in my town of Wyoming, Pennsylvania," she says.

Most Baltimore Albums are predominantly red and green, but Cheryl, who loves color, used a rainbow of colors in her quilt. She also used

16" blocks, rather than the 12" blocks frequently seen in modern Baltimore Albums.

This is the second in a series of four Baltimore Albums that Cheryl has made.

Peaceable Kingdom
1996

The paintings of the 18th-century artist Edward Hicks inspired many of the images in this quilt. Others came from rubbings from cemetery headstones in the historic Forty Fort Cemetery at Forty Fort, Pennsylvania.

"The vase and most of the leaves are based on the rubbings," says Cheryl. "The fruit and flowers in the vase are reminiscent of 18th-century crewel work."

The appliqués are cut mostly from plaid fabrics and stitched to a background of unbleached muslin.

"It's quilted heavily," notes Cheryl, "using 1,000 yards of quilting thread."

Hollis Chatelain
Hillsborough, North Carolina

*H*ollis Chatelain had worked in different areas of the art field for 15 years before becoming a quilter.

"I discovered textiles while living in Africa," says Hollis. "I decided to learn to sew and quilt because I was fascinated by the beauty and richness of African fabrics."

"In the Sahel, the baobab tree is considered the tree of life."

That was six years ago, and since then Hollis has made fabric her medium of choice for creative expression. Working 60 hours a week in her studio, she has completed more than 100 quilts, all of them original works. The techniques she uses most often are machine piecing and dye painting.

"I love the texture and warmth of fabric, and I like all the different aspects of creating a quilt," says Hollis. "Quilting is the one art form that has fulfilled and challenged my artistic quest."

Sahel won first place in pictorial quilts in the 1998 American Quilter's Society Quilt Show in Paducah, Kentucky.

Sahel
1997

"Living for eight years in the Sahel, I grew to love and admire the nomads who live there," says Hollis Chatelain.

The Sahel is the semiarid region of Africa between the Sahara to the north and the savannas to the south.

"In the Sahel, the baobab tree is considered the tree of life," she continues. Having photographed and drawn these magnificent trees for years, Hollis decided to make the baobab the central focus of this quilted tribute.

This dye-painted masterpiece has won several awards, including a second place and Viewer's Choice at Houston and Best of Show at the Durham Arts Guild Show in Durham, North Carolina.

Hollis Chatelain drew inspiration for this quilt from photographs she took while living in West Africa. Appliqué and dye painting are her techniques of choice.

Michele Hardy
Mandeville, Louisiana

I like to work intuitively, letting the materials and colors inspire me. And I love color—bright, saturated, intense, vibrant colors. I don't do brown." Michele enjoys machine work— machine appliqué, thread embellishment, and free-motion machine quilting. "I love the speed of a great computerized sewing machine and the special effects I can create."

"I don't do brown."

A glance at one of Michele's quilts, like *Daystar*, assures you she's sincere when she says, "I truly believe that art should be fun. My images, whether abstract or representational, are always happy ones, coming from the joy that I get from quilting."

Daystar
1996

Michele made this quilt as a tribute to her grandmother, Stella Laferriere, who passed away in 1996.

"Mem, as she was known, taught me how to sew and appreciate beautiful fabric," says Michele.

Michele chose the image of the bright, rising sun— complete with smiling face— and interpreted it in the rich, vibrant colors that her grandmother loved.

"*Daystar* is a celebration of life," says Michele.

Hand-dyed fabrics, shiny rayon thread, and Michele's enchanting design combine to prove this quilter's philosophy that art should be fun.

138

Mary Grace Brown
Birmingham, Alabama

Mary Grace Brown had dabbled a bit in quilting since the early 1970s. "But I didn't get serious about it until 1987 when I attended my first IQA (International Quilter's Association) show in Houston," she says, "and later the AQS (American Quilter's Society) show in Paducah. Seeing what was happening in the quilting world inspired me to do more involved quilts."

Mary Grace's quilts are very involved indeed; she spends many, many hours producing each masterpiece. And her efforts have not gone unrecognized. She has won numerous awards in not only local quilt shows but also in national competition. Several of her quilts have been accepted into both the Houston and Paducah shows; she won second place for large appliquéd quilts in Houston in 1996. In 1997, that same quilt was exhibited at quilt shows in England, Scotland, and the Netherlands.

My Blue Heaven *is a study in Feathered Stars. Its maker, Mary Grace Brown, was inspired to create it by the work of Marsha McCloskey.*

My Blue Heaven
1993

Many quilters hesitate to tackle the intricate piecing of a Feathered Star. Not Mary Grace Brown. In fact, she tackled nine different versions of the block to make *My Blue Heaven*, which was inspired by a Feathered Star sampler by Marsha McCloskey.

Her stars were a success, with clean lines and sharp points. The serenity of her color choice gives a calmness and continuity to the complexity of the block designs. *My Blue Heaven* has won several ribbons in local quilt shows, and in 1995, it was juried into the AQS show in Paducah.

139

Quilt Smart Workshop
A Guide to Quiltmaking

Preparing Fabric

Before cutting out any pieces, be sure to wash and dry your fabric to preshrink it. All-cotton fabrics may need to be pressed before cutting. Trim selvages from the fabric before you cut your pieces.

Making Templates

Before you can make some of the quilts in this book, you must make templates from the printed pattern pieces given. Quilters have used many materials to make templates, including cardboard and sandpaper. Transparent template plastic, available at craft supply and quilt shops, is durable, see-through, and easy to use.

To make templates using plastic, place the plastic sheet on the printed page and trace the pattern piece, using a laundry marker or permanent fine-tip marking pen. For machine piecing, trace along the outside solid (cutting) line. For hand piecing, trace along the inside broken (stitching) line. Cut out the template along the traced line. Label each template with the pattern name, letter, grain line arrow, and match points (corner dots).

Marking and Cutting Fabric

Place the template facedown on the wrong side of the fabric and mark around the template with a sharp pencil. Move the template (see next two paragraphs) and continue marking pieces; mark several before you stop to cut.

If you will be piecing your quilt by machine, the pencil lines represent the cutting lines. Leave about ¼" between pieces as you mark. Cut along the marked lines.

For hand piecing, the pencil lines are the seam lines. Leave at least ¾" between marked lines for seam allowances. Add ¼" seam allowance around each piece as you cut. Mark match points (corner dots) on each piece.

Hand Piecing

To hand piece, place two fabric pieces together with right sides facing. Insert a pin in each match point of the top piece. Stick the pin through both pieces and check to be sure that it pierces the match point on the bottom piece (*Figure 1*). Adjust the pieces if necessary to align the match points. (The raw edges of the two pieces may not be exactly aligned.) Pin the pieces securely together.

Sew with a running stitch of 8 to 10 stitches per inch. Checking your stitching as you go to be sure that you are stitching in the seam line of both pieces, sew from match point to match point. To make sharp corners, begin and end the stitching exactly at the match point; do not stitch into the seam allowances. When joining units where several seams come together, do not sew over seam allowances; sew through them at the point where all seam lines meet (*Figure 2*).

Always press both seam allowances to one side. Pressing the seam open, as in dressmaking, may leave gaps between the stitches through which quilt batting may beard. Press seam allowances toward the darker fabric whenever you can. When four or more seams meet at one point, such as at the corner of a block, press all the seams in a "swirl" in the same direction to reduce bulk (*Figure 3*).

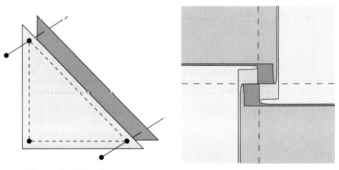

Figure 1–Aligning Match Points

Figure 3–Pressing Intersecting Seams

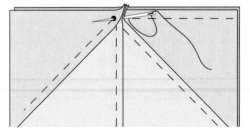

Figure 2–Joining Units

Machine Piecing

To machine piece, place two fabric pieces together with right sides facing. Align match points as described under "Hand Piecing" and pin the pieces together securely.

Set your stitch length at 12 to 15 stitches per inch. At this setting, you will not need to backstitch to lock seam beginnings and ends. Use a presser foot that gives a perfect ¼" seam allowance, or measure ¼" from the sewing machine needle and mark that point on the presser foot with nail polish or masking tape.

Chain-piece sections, stitching edge to edge, to save time when sewing similar sets of pieces (*Figure 4*). Join the first two pieces as usual. At the end of the seam, do not backstitch, cut the thread, or lift the presser foot. Instead, sew a few stitches off the fabric. Place the next two pieces and continue stitching. Keep sewing until all the sets are joined. Then cut the sets apart.

Press seam allowances toward the darker fabric. When you join blocks or rows, press the seam allowances of the top piece in one direction and the seam allowances of the bottom piece in the opposite direction to help ensure that the seams will lie flat (*Figure 5*).

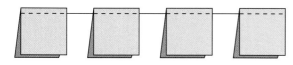

Figure 4–Chain Piecing

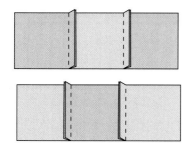

Figure 5–Pressing Seams for Machine Piecing

Hand Appliqué

Hand appliqué is the best way to achieve the look of traditional appliqué. However, using freezer paper, which is sold in grocery stores, can save a lot of time because it eliminates the need for hand basting the seam allowances.

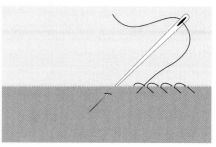

Figure 6–Slipstitch

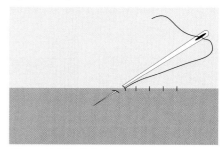

Figure 7–Blindstitch

Make templates without seam allowances. Trace the template onto the *dull* side of the freezer paper and cut the paper on the marked line. Make a freezer-paper shape for each piece to be appliquéd. Pin the freezer-paper shape, with its *shiny side up*, to the *wrong side* of your fabric. Following the paper shape and adding a scant ¼" seam allowance, cut out the fabric piece. Do not remove the pins. Using the tip of a hot, dry iron, press the seam allowance to the shiny side of the freezer paper. Be careful not to touch the shiny side of the freezer paper with the iron. Remove the pins.

Pin the appliqué shape in place on the background fabric. Use one strand of sewing thread in a color to match the appliqué shape. Using a very small slipstitch (*Figure 6*) or blindstitch (*Figure 7*), appliqué the shape to the background fabric.

After your stitching is complete, cut away the background fabric behind the appliqué shape, leaving ¼" seam allowance. Separate the freezer paper from the fabric with your fingernail and pull gently to remove it.

Mitering Borders

Mitered borders take a little extra care to construct. First, measure your quilt. Cut two border strips to fit the shorter of two opposite sides, plus the width of the border plus 2". Now center the measurement for the shorter side on one border strip and place a pin at each end of the measurement. Match the pins on the border strip to the corners of the longer side of the quilt. Join the border strip to the quilt, easing the quilt to fit between the pins and stopping ¼" from each corner of the quilt (*Figure 8*). Join the remaining cut strip to the opposite end of the quilt. Cut and join the remaining borders in the same manner. Press seams to one side. Follow *Figures 9 and 10* to miter corners.

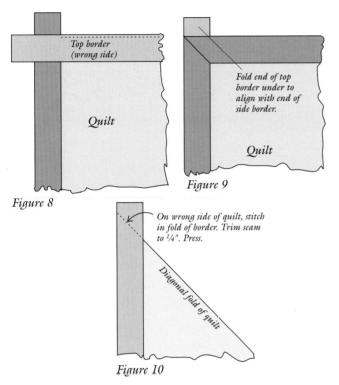

Figure 8

Figure 9

Figure 10

Mitering Borders

Marking Your Quilt Top

After the quilt top is completed, it should be thoroughly pressed and then marked with quilting designs. The most popular methods for marking use stencils or templates. Both can be purchased, or you can make your own. Use a silver quilter's pencil for marking light to medium fabrics and a white artist's pencil on dark fabrics. Lightly mark the quilt top with your chosen quilting designs.

Making a Backing

While some fabric and quilt shops sell 90" and 108" widths of backing fabric, the instructions in *Great American Quilts* give backing yardage based on 45"-wide fabric. When using 45"-wide fabric, all quilts wider than 42" will require a pieced backing. For quilts whose width measures between 42" and 80", purchase an amount of fabric equal to two times the desired length of the unfinished quilt backing. (The unfinished quilt backing should be at least 3" larger on all sides than the quilt top.)

The backing fabric should be of a type and color that is compatible with the quilt top. Percale sheets are not recommended, because they are tightly woven and difficult to hand-quilt through.

A pieced backing for a bed quilt should have three panels. The three-panel backing is recommended because it tends to wear better and lie flatter than the two-panel type, the center seam of which often makes a ridge down the center of the quilt. Begin by cutting the fabric in half widthwise (*Figure 11*). Open the two lengths and stack them, with right sides facing and selvages aligned. Stitch along both selvage edges to create a tube of fabric (*Figure 12*). Cut down the center of the top layer of fabric *only* and open the fabric flat (*Figure 13*).

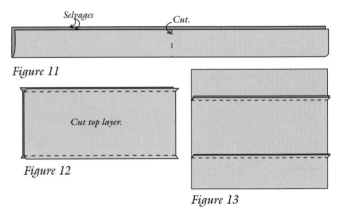

Figure 11

Figure 12

Figure 13

Making a Three-Panel Backing

Layering and Basting

Prepare a working surface to spread out the quilt. Place the backing on the working surface right side down. Unfold the batting and place it on top of the backing. Smooth any wrinkles or lumps in the batting.

Lay the quilt top right side up on top of the batting and backing. Make sure the backing and quilt top are aligned. Knot a long strand of sewing thread and use a darning needle for basting. Begin basting in the center of your quilt and baste out toward the edges. The stitches should cover an ample amount of the quilt so that the layers do not shift during quilting. Inadequate basting can result in puckers and folds on the back and front of the quilt.

Hand Quilting

Hand quilting can be done with the quilt in a hoop or in a floor frame. It is best to start quilting in the middle of your quilt and work out toward the edges.

Most quilters use a very thin, short needle called a "between." Betweens are available in sizes 7 to 12, with 7 being the longest and 12 the shortest. If you are a beginning quilter, try a size 7 or 8. Because betweens are so much shorter than other hand-sewing needles, they may feel awkward at first. As your skill increases, try switching to a smaller needle to help you make smaller stitches.

Quilting thread, heavier and stronger than ordinary sewing thread, is available in a wide variety of colors. But if color matching is critical and you can't find the color you need, you may substitute cotton sewing thread. We suggest you coat it with beeswax before quilting to prevent it from tangling and knotting.

To begin, thread your needle with an 18" to 24" length and make a small knot at one end. Insert the needle into the top of the quilt approximately ½" from the point you want to begin quilting. Do not take the needle through all three layers, but stop it in the batting and bring it up through the quilt top again at your starting point. Tug gently on the thread to pop the knot through the quilt top into the batting. This anchors the thread without an unsightly knot showing on the back. With your non-sewing hand underneath the quilt, insert the needle with the point straight down in the quilt about ¹⁄₁₆" from the starting point. With your underneath finger, feel for the point as the needle comes through the backing (*Figure 14*). Place the thumb of your sewing hand approximately ½" ahead of your needle. At the moment you feel the needle touch your underneath finger, push the fabric up from below as you rock the needle down to a nearly horizontal position. Using the thumb of your sewing hand in conjunction with the underneath hand, pinch a little hill in the fabric and push the tip of the needle back through the quilt top (*Figure 15*).

Now either push the needle all the way through to complete one stitch or rock the needle again to an upright position on its point to take another stitch. Take no more than a quarter-needleful of stitches before pulling the needle through.

When you have about 6" of thread remaining, you must end the old thread securely and invisibly. Carefully tie a knot in the thread, flat against the surface of the fabric. Pop the knot through the top as you did when beginning the line of quilting. Clip the thread, rethread your needle, and continue quilting.

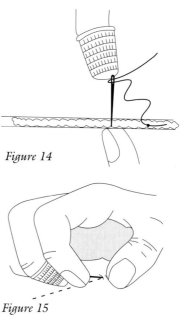

Figure 14

Figure 15

Hand Quilting

Machine Quilting

Machine quilting is as old as the sewing machine itself; but until recently, it was thought inferior to hand quilting. Machine quilting does, however, require a different set of skills from hand quilting.

Machine quilting can be done on your sewing machine using a straight, even stitch and a special presser foot. A walking foot, or even-feed foot, is recommended for straight-line machine quilting to help the top fabric move through the machine at the same rate that the feed dogs move the bottom fabric. With free-motion machine quilting, use a darning foot to protect your fingers and to prevent skipped stitches.

Regular sewing thread or nylon thread can be used for machine quilting. With the quilt top facing you, roll the long edges of the basted quilt toward the center of the quilt, leaving a 12"-wide area unrolled in the center. Secure the roll with bicycle clips, metal bands that are available at quilt shops.

Begin at one unrolled end and fold the quilt over and over until only a small area is showing. This will be the area where you will begin to machine quilt.

Place the folded portion of the quilt in your lap. Start machine quilting in the center and work to the right side of the quilt, unfolding and unrolling the quilt as you go. Remove the quilt from the machine, turn it, and reinsert it in the machine to stitch the left side. A table placed behind your sewing machine will help support the quilt as it is stitched.

Curves and circles are most easily made by free-motion machine quilting. Using a darning foot and with the feed dogs down, move the quilt under the needle with movements of your fingertips. Place your fingertips on the fabric on each side of the presser foot and run your machine at a steady, medium speed. The length of the stitches is determined by the rate of speed at which you move fabric through the machine. Do not rotate the quilt; rather, move it from side to side as needed. Always stop with the needle down to keep the quilt from shifting.

Making Binding

A continuous bias strip is frequently used by quilters for all kinds of quilts but is especially recommended for quilts with curved edges. Follow these steps to make a continuous bias strip:

1. To make continuous bias binding, you'll need a square of fabric. Multiply the number of inches of binding needed by the desired width of the binding (usually 2¼"). Use a calculator to find the square root of that number. That's the size square needed to make your binding.

2. Cut the square in half diagonally.

3. With right sides facing, join triangles to form a sawtooth as shown in *Figure 16*.

4. Press seam open. Mark off parallel lines the desired width of the binding as shown in *Figure 17*.

5. With right sides facing, align raw edges marked Seam 2. As you align edges, extend a Seam 2 point past its natural matching point by the distance of the width of the bias strip as shown in *Figure 18*. Join.

6. Cut the binding in a continuous strip, starting with the protruding point and following the marked lines around the tube.

7. Press the binding strip in half lengthwise, with wrong sides facing. This gives you double fold, or French-fold, binding, which is sturdier than single-fold binding.

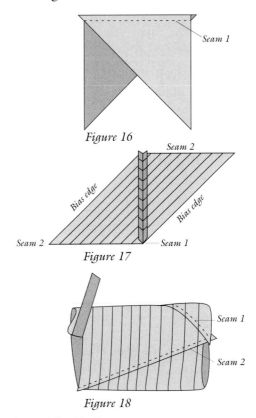

Figure 16

Figure 17

Figure 18

Continuous Bias Binding

Attaching Binding

Trim the backing and batting even with the edge of the quilt top. Beginning at the midpoint of one side of the quilt, pin the binding to the top, with right sides facing and raw edges aligned.

Stitch the binding along one edge of the quilt, sewing through all layers. Backstitch at the beginning of the seam to lock the stitching.

Stop stitching ¼" from the corner and backtack. Clip the threads and remove the quilt from the machine. Fold the binding straight up, away from the corner, and make a 45° fold. Bring the binding straight down, aligning with the next edge to be sewn. Inside the fold is an angled pleat extending from the corner. Continue stitching around the edge. Join the beginning and ending of the binding strip by machine.

Turn the binding to the back side and blindstitch in place. At each corner, fold the excess binding neatly and blindstitch in place, to resemble a miter. Slipstitch corner folds closed.